THE INTERSTICES REQUIRED FOR THE PROMOTION TO ORDERS

THE CATHOLIC UNIVERSITY OF AMERICA
CANON LAW STUDIES
No. 196

The Interstices Required for the Promotion to Orders

BY

REV. JOHN MARK GANNON, S.T.L., J.C.L.
PRIEST OF THE DIOCESE OF ERIE

A DISSERTATION

SUBMITTED TO THE FACULTY OF THE SCHOOL OF CANON LAW OF THE CATHOLIC UNIVERSITY OF AMERICA IN PARTIAL FULFILLMENT OF THE REQUIREMENTS FOR THE DEGREE OF DOCTOR OF CANON LAW

THE CATHOLIC UNIVERSITY OF AMERICA PRESS
WASHINGTON, D. C.
1944

NIHIL OBSTAT:

Hieronymus D. Hannan, M.A., Ll.B., S.T.D., J.C.D.
Censor Deputatus.
Washingtonii, D. C., die 15 Maii, 1944.

IMPRIMATUR:

✠ Joannes Marcus Gannon, D.D.,
Episcopus Eriensis.
Erie, Pa., die 17 Maii, 1944.

Murray & Heister
Washington, D. C.

Printed by
Times and News Publishing Co.
Gettysburg, Pa., U. S. A.

In Honor of Mary,
Mother of God

INTRODUCTION

The interstices are those intervals of time which by the law of the Church are to be observed in connection with the conferring of orders.[1] Although the practice of observing the interstices was not uniform at all times or in all places, nevertheless from the first centuries certain intervals were sustained by universal law and custom.

The earliest legislation was enacted by the Council of Sardica (343).[2] This legislation was approved by the Roman Pontiffs Siricius (385)[3] and Gelasius I (494).[4]

Gelasius was the first to use the term as we have it today.[5]

The Church adopted the interstices for a twofold purpose: first, that a cleric exercise the order received; and secondly, that he prove himself worthy of receiving higher orders.[6]

Saint Paul, in speaking of the qualities of a Bishop, made clear his view on the matter of interstices when he wrote: "He must not be a new convert, lest he be puffed up with pride and incur the condemnation passed on the devil."[7] Saint Paul implied in this text that an aspirant should be tried and proved at each step

---

[1] "Interstitia nihil aliud sunt quam illud intervallum temporum quod ex Ecclesiae constitutione interiacere debet inter susceptionem unius et alterius ordinis."—Ferraris (✠ ca. 1763), *Prompta Bibliotheca, Canonica, Juridica, Moralis Theologica, necnon Ascetica, Polemica, Rubricistica, Historica* (9 vols., Romae, 1885-1899), s.v. "Interstitia," n. 1.

[2] C. 10, D. LXI.

[3] C. 3, D. LXXVII; Jaffé, *Regesta Pontificum Romanorum ab condita Ecclesia ad annum post Christum natum MCXCVIII* (Editionem secundam correctam et auctam auspiciis Gulielmi Wattenbach curaverunt S. Loewenfeld, F. Kaltenbrunner, P. Ewald, 2 vols. in 1, Lipsiae, 1885-1888), n. 255. (Hereafter cited as Jaffé.)

[4] C. 9, D. LXXVII; Jaffé, n. 636.

[5] ". . . quorum annorum fuerant interstitia collatura." C. 9, D. LXXVII; Jaffé, n. 636.

[6] Sebastianelli (✠ 1916), *Praelectiones Iuris Canonici, De Personis* (2. ed., Romae: Pustet, 1905), p. 197.

[7] I Timothy, iii, 6.

in advancement to the episcopate, so that there would be in the candidate no lack of the virtue or of the learning which could be acquired only through time and experience. He warned that one who attained such a high place among men without the benefit of experience and understanding might easily fall a prey to pride upon finding himself so elevated without effort on his own part and without time for the due appreciation of his responsibilities.

The interstices are considered necessary for admission to the sacramental gift of the priesthood as probationary steps. The ascending orders are not regarded here, under the aspect of the interstices, as participating steps in that great gift.

TABLE OF CONTENTS

CHAPTER I

The Law of Interstices Before the Council of Trent

ARTICLE 1. OBLIGATION TO OBSERVE THE INTERSTICES

The subject of interstices in the early Church resolved itself into two questions: first, what were the interstices among the orders determined by canonical rules; second, whether occasionally some of the major orders were omitted with the consequence that priests were ordained without having received the diaconate, or that Bishops were consecrated who had never been ordained priests.

The Council of Sardica (343) ruled that no one be raised to the episcopate until he had filled the office of lector, deacon, and priest, and so by slow and moderate steps had prepared his way for a competent fulfillment of the episcopal functions.[1]

It seems certain that the particle *aut* in canon 13 of the Council of Sardica has the same value as the conjunction *et*. There would have been no reason for placing the order of diaconate on a parity with the priesthood as a prerequisite for the episcopate; otherwise, what would there have been to prevent the elimination of the order of priesthood itself? Yet that would have been absurd.[2]

It follows, therefore, that the two questions proposed above were decided by the Council of Sardica, for it directed that the interstices were to be closely observed; and it also demanded that the office of priesthood was to be given only to a deacon, and that the episcopate should not be conferred except to priests.

---

[1] Can. 13: ". . . ut non prius ordinetur, nisi antea lectoris munere, et officio diaconi aut presbyteri fuerit perfunctus, et ita per singulos gradus (si dignus fuerit) ascendat ad culmen episcopatus."—C. 10, D. LXI.

[2] Thomassinus (1619-1695), *Vetus et Nova Ecclesiae Disciplina circa Beneficia et Beneficiarios* (10 vols., Magontiaci, 1787), P. I, lib. II, cap. XXXVI, n. 2.

The time that was to elapse between the orders was not determined, but the Council insisted that the candidates for the episcopate remain in lower orders as lectors, deacons, and priests as long as prudence required it to have their faith, morals, and character put to a sufficient test. Every virtue fitting the episcopate was to be developed before the candidate was to be accepted. This necessitated intervals between the stages of advancement in order that the candidate might acquire that virtue and knowledge.

The second canon of the I General Council of Nicaea (325) ordained that no neophyte was to raised to the episcopate forthwith, but that he should pass through a period of probation for the testing of his worthiness.[3]

It is true that the necessity for priestly administration has prompted the Church from the earliest times to be most generous in cases of necessity as to the relaxation of the requirements for ordination. The occasions for these dispensations will be observed later. It will serve here to recall the assertion of the I General Council of Nicaea that many things, whether through necessity or for other adequate reasons, were done in opposition to the law, such as the ordaining to the priesthood or the consecrating of men lately converted from paganism. The Council deplored the fact that the urgent need for priests and Bishops hastened the conferring of Baptism on men while they were still in the course of instruction, and then bore them forthwith into the priesthood and episcopacy. The glossator Joannes Teutonicus (✠ 1245), in commenting on this procedure, offered as an explanation the rule of law that what is not licit in law necessity makes licit.[4] Such an unqualified generality was not, then as now, without its possible element of danger; nevertheless in this as in other matters it could find a useful application.

The Council continued that, although this course was justifiable in the past, there was no such emergency present in its own time, and the natural procedure by certain steps should be the

---

[3] C. 1, D. XLVIII.

[4] "Si propter necessitatem aliquid fit, videtur quod illud licite fit: quia quod non est licitum in lege, necessitas facit licitum."—*Glossa Ordinaria*, ad c. 1, D. XLVIII, s. v. *necessitatem;* C. 4, X, *de regulis iuris*, V, 41.

rule again. This meant that the convert should be fully instructed and prepared for Baptism, and then pass through the usual periods of probation before attaining the episcopate. The Council herein followed the caution of Saint Paul, who exhorted a careful and gradual approach to the priesthood and the episcopacy, lest the convert become proud and fall away.[5]

The glossator observed soundly that a man who found himself in the priesthood prematurely did not approve and appreciate the means of self-humiliation, was ignorant of the manners of the faithful, did not fast, weep, correct himself, or show himself sympathetic to the poor.[6]

Thus far, one is satisfied that the Church at her institution and during her early development was well aware that the importance of each order was to be weighed carefully, and that the orders were to be received in proper sequence in order that the candidate might grasp the loftiness of the ministry to which he was called.

Pope Siricius (385) defined the required intervals a little more precisely, although he asserted no more than what was the custom which the Council of Sardica presupposed to be widespread and observed by all.[7] Siricius was in favor of an early ordination to the lectorate. He decreed that the order of lector should be conferred before the age of puberty had been reached.[8]

There was a difference of opinion among the glossators as to the age of puberty. Huguccio (✠ 1210) held that this period of life was reached with the twelfth year. Bartholomew of Brescia (✠ 1258) advanced the view that what Huguccio accepted was not true in the case of boys, but was tenable as to the age of puberty for girls. Joannes Teutonicus (✠ 1245) accepted fourteen years as the age of puberty. This factor was important for the ascertaining of the ages for the various minor orders.[9]

---

[5] I Timothy, iii, 6.

[6] *Principium,* D. XLVIII.

[7] C. 3, D. LXXVII; Jaffé, n. 255.

[8] "Quicumque itaque se ecclesiae vovit obsequiis a sua infantia, ante pubertatis annos baptizari et lectorum debet ministerio sociari."—C. 3, D. LXXVII; Jaffé, n. 255.

[9] *Glossa Ordinaria,* s. v. *pubertatis,* C. 3, D. LXXVII.

According to Pope Siricius, during the interval from puberty to the age of twenty years, the cleric was to receive the orders of an acolyte and subdeacon. Siricius authorized this procedure for all clerics, whether they had taken wives or had preferred to remain celibate.[10] The glossator, in discussing the inclusion by Pope Siricius of subdeacons in this category, stated that subdiaconate was not a sacred order in Siricius' time, and accordingly there was no necessity for celibacy.

Those who had completed the twentieth year were to undergo a further period of probation before receiving the diaconate.[11] The provision as to the duration of the period was not clear.

Between the diaconate, however, and the priesthood, Siricius required a definite interlude of five years.[12]

Siricius then indicated a ten-year interval before the office of Bishop could be attained.[13]

Did the total of these computations make an aggregate of thirty or thirty-six years as the age for promotion to the episcopate? If one favors thirty-six years, then even after ordination to the priesthood one did not prove himself worthy for the episcopate until he had extended his probation another ten years. Huguccio felt that these ten years were to be computed as beginning from the twentieth year, the age given above in reference to the subdiaconate. Therefore, shortly after the reception of the priesthood one could be consecrated a Bishop.[14]

Those who dedicated themselves to the service of the Church at an adult age, however, could not be expected to submit to such an extended "novitiate."[15] The Pontiff was indulgent with this

---

[10] "Qui ab accessu adolescentiae usque ad vigesimum aetatis annum si probabiliter vixerit, una tantum, et ea, quam virginem communi per sacerdotem benedictione perceperit, uxore contentus; acolythus et subdiaconus esse debebit. . . ."—C. 3, D. LXXVII; Jaffé, n. 255.

[11] ". . . posteaque ad diaconii gradum (si se ipsum primitus, continentia praeeunte, dignum probaverit) accedat."—C. 3, D. LXXVII; Jaffé, n. 255.

[12] "Ubi si ultra quinque annos laudabiliter ministraverit, congrue presbyterium consequatur."—C. 3, LXXVII; Jaffé, n. 255.

[13] "Exinde post decennium episcopalem cathedram poterit adipisci. . . ."—C. 3, D. LXXVII; Jaffé, n. 255.

[14] *Glossa Ordinaria,* s. v. *exinde,* C. 3, D. LXXVII.

[15] C. 3, D. LXXVII; Jaffé, n. 255.

class of candidates, explaining that if the time of probation were not shortened, their desire might never be realized.

The glossator indicated two stages in life as representing adult age, one at twenty-three and the other at thirty years of age. This, of course, did not interfere with the interstices which were to follow, but certainly the determining of the adult age furnished the starting point from which the interstices were to be reckoned.

The interstices were so arranged that an adult could receive every order over a span of shortly more than seven years. During the first term of two years the candidate received the orders of lector and exorcist.[16] The aspirant then proceeded within five years to the reception of the orders of an acolyte and subdeacon. Shortly afterwards he was admitted to the order of a deacon. After serving another apprenticeship he was promoted to the priesthood, and even to the episcopate if he was found deserving.[17]

Rufinus (✠ ca. 1190)) commented that the *quinquennium aliud* was to be calculated from the completion of the two years previously mentioned, making a total of seven years.[18]

As shall be remarked later in this study, religious conspicuous for their sanctity merited a mitigation of the canons, and the time of the interstices was reduced for them. Siricius, however, did not dispense religious. He asserted that they were to be given minor orders before the thirtieth year. Then they could be promoted to the order of diaconate, and afterwards to the order of priesthood, but he upheld the interstices of five years between diaconate and priesthood, and ten years between priesthood and the episcopate, and decreed that they be strictly observed.[19]

Pope Zosimus (418) was no less insistent that a path leading to such high responsibility should be journeyed slowly, and he

[16] ". . . desiderii sui fructum non aliter obtinebit, nisi eo quo baptizatur tempore statim lectorum aut exorcistarum numero societur. . . ."—C. 3, D. LXXVII; Jaffé, n. 255.

[17] ". . . expleto biennio, per quinquennium aliud acolythus et subdiaconus fiat, et sic ad diaconatum . . . provehatur. Exinde iam accessu temporum presbyterio vel episcopatui . . . non immerito societur."—C. 3, D. LXXVII; Jaffé, n. 255.

[18] *Summa Decretorum* (ed. H. Singer, Paderborn, 1902), C. 3, D. LXXVII.

[19] C. 29, C. XVI, q. I; Jaffé, n. 255.

ordained that all the required steps must be taken, so that no one should dare set foot in the ministry until the canons regarding the interstices were fulfilled.[20]

He reminded the Bishops that if the offices of the secular curia were given through merit and only after a rigorous apprenticeship, how much more discriminating should the Church be when inviting its candidates to assume the responsibility of ecclesiastical leadership. He bade them to let the aspirant acquire a knowledge of the elements of the functions of divine service, and the candidate was not to think it beneath his dignity to become an exorcist, acolyte, subdeacon and deacon successively and in season, and only then to reach the goal of the priesthood when his age corresponded to the name of presbyter, and his personal services attested the merit of his uprightness.[21]

Pope Celestine I (428) in a letter to the Bishops of Gaul, protested vigorously against the conferring of orders without the observance of the intervals of time.[22] Proceeding in accord with the argument of Zosimus, he said that in every human institution the candidate advanced only by successive steps and degrees to the highest position. The Pontiff inquired whether the priesthood, a divine institution, alone among institutions was of such small value that it might be bestowed with greater ease, even though its responsibilities were fulfilled with only greater difficulty. Then he enacted the law that anyone who had not risen through each branch of service and at the approved time could not be allowed to attain the priesthood.

Pope Zosimus in a letter to Hesychius described definite intervals to be observed for each order.[23] He wrote of one who devoted himself to the ecclesiastical ministry from infancy.[24] The glossator asserted that the expression, *ab infantia,* referred to one who had reached the seventh year of age. The phrase,

---

[20] C. 2, D. LIX; Jaffé, n. 339.

[21] C. 2, D. LIX; Jaffé, n. 339.

[22] C. 4, D. LIX; Jaffé, n. 369.

[23] "In singulis gradibus haec tempora sunt observanda. . . ."—C. 2, D. LXXVII; Jaffé, n. 339.

[24] ". . . si ab infantia ecclesiasticis ministeriis nomen dederit. . . ."—C. 2, D. LXXVII; Jaffé, n. 339.

ecclesiasticis ministeriis nomen dederit, is not quite clear. It does not appear to refer to an actual formula of induction, but merely to an enrollment in the respective churches.[25]

According to Zosimus the first group of minor orders, namely, of lector and of exorcist, could be conferred in the interval between the ages of seven and twelve years. After the twelfth year one could receive the order of acolyte, but not until one had reached the age of twenty-one years was he to receive the order of a subdeacon.[26] The age for subdiaconate was not given directly, but the gloss held the opinion that the fourteen years' interval was to be computed from the age of seven years, which was apparent from the following chapter in the Decree of Gratian in which it was specified that subdiaconate be conferred in the twenty-first year.[27]

Zosimus proceeded with the indication that in the twenty-fifth year the cleric was given the diaconate, and after the thirtieth year of age the priesthood.[28] After the reception of the priesthood the candidate for the episcopacy had to prove his worth by superior standards. To qualify, he had to reflect in his life a profounder moral character and commendable wisdom.[29] There was no mention of tonsure, for at that time it was given with the first minor order.

It appears that the Popes divided the minor orders into two classes: in the first there were the orders of exorcist and lector, and in the second the orders of acolyte and subdeacon. There is no mention of the order of porter, and the order of a subdeacon

---

[25] *Glossa Ordinaria,* s. v. *nomen,* C. 2, D. LXXVII, referring to c. 21, D. L.

[26] ". . . ut inter lectores et exorcistas quinquennio teneatur, exinde acolitus vel subdiaconus quatordecim annis fiat. . . ."—C. 2, D. LXXVII; Jaffé, n. 339.

[27] C. 3, D. LXXVII; Jaffé, n. 255.

[28] ". . . et sic ad benedictionem diaconatus, si meretur, accedat, in quo ordine quinque annis, si inculpate gesserit, adherere debebit."—C. 2, D. LXXVII; Jaffé, n. 339.

[29] "Exinde suffragantibus stipendiis, per tot gradus datis propriae fidei documentis, sacerdotium poterit promereri, de quo loco, si eum exactior vita ad bonos mores perduxerit, summum pontificatum sperare debebit."—C. 2, D. LXXVII; Jaffé, n. 339.

is always numbered with that of the clerics in minor orders. Accordingly, it is noticed that the Pontiffs did not wish all minor orders to be conferred simultaneously. No one was to be advanced to the second category of minor orders until he had equipped himself spiritually and intellectually, and proved himself fit and worthy.

ARTICLE 2. EXCEPTIONS

As was observed above,[30] exceptions were occasionally allowed for some urgent cause. According to the Roman use, permission was granted in special cases to advance a subdeacon to the diaconate and presbyterate on the same day, lest having become a deacon, he should afterwards refuse to be advanced to the presbyterate. Pope Gelasius I (494) permitted subdeacons to be ordained priests if deacons refused the promotion intended for them.[31] This of course was a local relaxation, not a general standard.

Conditions created by war and famine in some provinces of Italy obliged Gelasius to reduce temporarily the intervals between orders to a period of three months. There were other cases mentioned in this canon, moreover, in the face of which the extraordinary merits of the subject or the need of the Church for administration justified a promotion to orders without the usual intervals.[32]

A religious, for instance, imbued with good moral habits and noted for his integrity of life if he desired to serve in the priesthood, could forthwith receive the order of lector.[33] The glossator commented that Gelasius allowed clerics and religious of certain provinces to be ordained because of a plague which was then current. There was a dearth of priests, and the people were suffering because of the consequent lack of ministers. Gelasius justified his action as not being an innovation by stating that the

[30] Cf. *supra*, pp. 2, 3.

[31] C. 9, D. LXXIV; Jaffé, n. 668.

[32] C. 9, D. LXXVII; Jaffé, n. 636.

[33] "Monachus vero novitius morum honestate fulcitus, continuo lector . . . effectus. . . ."—C. 9, D. LXXVII; Jaffé, n. 636.

ancient canons permitted such a reduction of the preparatory time-period in a case of necessity.[34]

After a lapse of three months the order of acolyte was conferred on the religious, especially when the consideration of more advanced years warranted such a step, and after another interval of three months the order of subdeacon was conferred. Three months later the cleric was made a deacon if he continued the manifestation of a virtuous life. After the completion of the year he was ordained to the priesthood.[35]

The glossator explained this action of the Pope by a similar exemption in the field of scholarship. He said that just as natural talents supply the difference of time in application and study to make one equally as well equipped as another, so do probity of life and virtue compensate for the youth of the candidate and the time ordinarily required to be spent in acquiring a priestly character; just as what is less equals that which is greater with due compensation.[36]

In granting this dispensation to laymen, Gelasius demanded compensations similar to those exacted of religious, namely, that they be men of integrity and learning.[37] He required that outstanding laymen spend not only a year in ascending the steps to the priesthood, as in the case of religious, but a half year in addition. Gelasius felt that some distinction had to be made between the religious life and life in the world, since the cloistered had already renounced and repudiated the pleasures of the world, and consequently were already advanced and tried and proven in virtue and wisdom.[38]

---

[34] C. 9, D. LXXVII; Jaffé, n. 636.

[35] ". . . post tres menses existat acolitus, maxime si huic etiam etas suffragatur; sexto mense subdiaconi nomen accipiat, ac si modestae conversationis honestaeque voluntatis existat, nono mense diaconus, completoque anno sit presbyter. . . ."—C. 9, D. LXXVII; Jaffé, n. 636.

[36] *Glossa Ordinaria,* ad c. 3, D. LXXVII, s. v. *devotio.*

[37] ". . . tantoque magis quod sacris aptum possit esse servitiis in eorum querendum est institutis, quantum de tempore, quo fuerint assequenda, decerpitur, ut morum hoc habere doceatur probitas, quod prolixior consuetudo non contulit. . . ."—C. 9, D. LXXVII; Jaffé, n. 636.

[38] "Quorum promotionibus super anni metas sex menses nihilominus subrogamus, quoniam, sicut dictum est, distare debet inter personam divino cultui deditam, et de laicorum conversatione venientem."—C. 9, D. LXXVII; Jaffé, n. 636.

The glossator, in commenting on this distinction between candidates coming from the religious and those from the lay life, deduced an analogy from court procedure. He remarked that if a lay person was cited to court for a deposition, he was examined more closely and with greater circumspection than a religious, for the reason that his life was not as well disciplined as the latter's, since he was less subject to vigilance from directive authority. Again, he argued that the testimony of four clerics was as weighty as that of six laymen, inasmuch as a cleric could advance as much in sincerity and truthfulness in a year's time as a layman could in a year and a half.[39]

Pope Gelasius reminded the Bishops that the dispensation which was issued because of conditions caused by a plague and famine was only of a temporary nature, and that after the normal situation was restored the law was to be observed.[40]

Gelasius' extraordinary concession did not, therefore, manifest the law as it then flourished, but served rather to demonstrate that outside an emergency the spirit of the ancient canons regarding the interstices was to be observed universally. For Gelasius concluded with the instruction that as soon as the immediate necessity for priests was supplied, the churches favored by this dispensation should revert to the general law of the period as representing the spirit of canonical tradition.

ARTICLE 3. SANCTIONS

There is evidence in the ante-Tridentine legislation that the intervals were to be observed strictly, and that the transgression of the law governing the intervals was corrected by ecclesiastical penalties. The Council of Constantinople (692) ruled that no one was to be ordained a subdeacon until the completion of the twentieth year, under the sanction that if any aspirant was ordained outside the regulated period he was to be deposed.[41]

[39] *Glossa Ordinaria,* ad c. 3, D. LXXVII, s. v. *examinari.*

[40] "Quae tamen eatenus indulgenda credimus ut ecclesiis ab hac occasione cessantibus canonum paternorum vetus forma servetur."—C. 9, D. LXXVII; Jaffé, n. 636.

[41] C. 4, D. LXXVII.

Clement III (1187-1191) at Rome suspended a cleric who, although he had received minor orders legitimately, was admitted to the subdiaconate and diaconate outside of the regulated period of time and without the observance of the intervals.[42] The Pontiff permitted him through the Bishop of Tours to exercise only the minor orders which had been lawfully conferred, and prescribed that in the meantime he should enter a monastery for penance and remain there until the Abbot saw fit to dispense him, and allow him to exercise the orders of the subdiaconate and the diaconate. Again, Clement III suspended three clerics who had received subdiaconate and diaconate "furtively," that is to say, they concealed the fact that they were being ordained out of season.[43] They were sentenced to do penance in a monastery until the Bishop granted a dispensation, and empowered them to exercise the functions of their orders.

The glossator added that without this dispensation they could not exercise the order received, or pass on to higher orders. They were considered suspended *a certis et definitis ordinibus exercendis.*[44]

---

[42] C. 2, X, *de eo qui furtive ordinem suscepit,* V, 30. In the Decretals it is ascribed to Celestine III (1191-1198)—Jaffé, n. 16, 603.

[43] C. 3, X, *de eo qui furtive ordinem suscepit,* V, 30; Jaffé, n. 16, 597.

[44] Cf. Canon 2279, § 2, 5°; *Glossa Ordinaria,* ad c. 3, X, *de eo qui furtive ordinem suscepit,* V, 30, s. v. *ministrare non debet* and *de nostra licentia.*

CHAPTER II

The Law of Interstices in the Council of Trent

ARTICLE 1. DECREES OF THE COUNCIL

A. The Nature and the End of the Law

The Council of Trent (1545-1563) ushered in a period noted for the improvement in general decisive legislation regarding the positive qualifications in the subject of ordination. Practically every aspect of the life of the candidate for orders was touched by the legislation of one or the other sessions of the Council. Viewing with alarm the notable lapse from the observance of regulations pertaining to the clerical order and life which was caused by the neglecting of the ancient canons on the clerical state, the Fathers of the Council wished to restate these canons and make new legislation where it was necessary.[1]

The Council of Trent prefaced its legislation on the interstices by stating the reasons why the candidates were to observe them, namely, ". . . that they may be taught more accurately how great is the burden of their vocation and may in accordance with the direction of the Bishop exercise themselves in each office . . . and thus they shall ascend step by step, that with increasing age they may grow in worthiness of life and in learning, which especially the example of their good conduct, their assiduous services in the Church, their greater reverence towards priests and the superior orders . . . will prove."[2]

The Provincial Councils of Halifax (1857)[3] and Westminster

[1] Conc. Trident., sess. XXIII, *de ref.*, c. 1; Schroeder, *Canons and Decrees of the Council of Trent: Original text with English translation* (B. Herder Book Co., St. Louis, 1941), p. 164. (Cited hereafter as Schroeder.)

[2] Conc. Trident., sess. XXIII, *de ref.*, c. 11; Schroeder, p. 171.

[3] "Serventur quoque interstitia ut uniuscujusque Ordinis officia clericus cognoscere et implere possit, antequam ad alium promoveatur."—*Acta et Decreta Sacrorum Conciliorum Recentiorum, Collectio Lacensis* (7 vols., Friburgi Brisgoviae, 1870-1890), III, 747, d. (Hereafter cited as *Coll. Lac.*)

(1852)[4] incorporated the reasons directly within their legislation on the interstices.

B. Interstices as Affecting Minor Orders

As to the intervals for minor orders, the Council of Trent decreed that "minor orders shall be conferred on those who understand at least the Latin language, observing the prescribed interstices, unless the Bishop should deem it more expedient to act otherwise. . . ."[5]

C. Interstices as Affecting Major Orders

Clerics in minor orders "shall not be promoted to sacred orders till a year after the reception of the last of the minor orders, unless necessity or the need of the Church shall in the judgment of the Bishop require otherwise."[6]

Concerning the interval before the diaconate, it was decreed that ". . . those who have been promoted to the sacred order of subdeacon shall not till they have completed at least one year therein be permitted to ascend to a higher order, unless the Bishop shall judge otherwise. Two sacred orders shall not be conferred on the same day, even to regulars, any privileges and indults whatsoever to whomsoever granted to the contrary notwithstanding."[7]

In regard to the order of priesthood, the Council resolved that "those who have conducted themselves piously and faithfully in their performance of earlier functions and are accepted for the order of priesthood, shall . . . be persons who . . . have served in the office of deacon for one entire year, unless by reason of the advantage and need of the Church, the Bishop should judge otherwise. . . ."[8]

---

[4] "Serventur, quantum fieri potest, interstitia, ut unusquisque, antequam ad altiorem gradum ascendat, ordinem jam susceptum exercendi opportunitatem frequenter habeat, sicque rubricas mature discat."—*Coll. Lac.*, III, 936, b.

[5] Conc. Trident., sess. XXIII, *de ref.*, c. 11; Schroeder, p. 171.

[6] Conc. Trident., sess. XXIII, *de ref.*, c. 11; Schroeder, p. 171.

[7] Conc. Trident., sess. XXIII, *de ref.*, c. 13; Schroeder, p. 172.

[8] Conc. Trident., sess. XXIII, *de ref.*, c. 14; Schroeder, p. 172.

ARTICLE 2. ANALYSIS OF CONCILIAR DECREES

A. Interstices as Affecting Minor Orders

Judging the law as fixed by the Council of Trent, it appears that no interstices were required for minor orders. The intervals for minor orders were not stated expressly, hence authors varied in their interpretations and opinions.[9] However, since the Council prescribed that the interstices for minor orders were to be observed unless the Bishop should deem it more expedient to act otherwise, it followed that tonsure and the four minor orders, or even the four minor orders alone, could not be conferred at one and the same time without a just cause.

---

[9] Gonzalez-Tellez (✠ ca. 1674) said that the Council of Trent did not specify any interstices for minor orders, yet did not expressly take them away—*Commentaria Perpetua in Singulos Textus Quinque Librorum Decretalium Gregorii IX* (5 vols., Venetiis, 1756), lib. I, tit. 11, cap. 15, n. 8; Fagnanus (1598-1678) asserted that the Bishop may confer four minor orders on one day, since the text of the Council of Trent spoke indeterminately, and so had to be understood as permitting the immediately consecutive conferring of all: "indefinita aequipollet universali"—*Jus Canonicum seu Commentaria Absolutissima in Quinque Libros Decretalium* (5 vols., Romae, 1661), II, *de temporibus ordinationum et qualitate ordinandorum,* cap. *De eo,* n. 8; according to Pirhing (1606-1679), it was left to the judgment of the Bishop to determine the interstices for minor orders, but he added that custom had to justify the procedure if all four were to be conferred on the same day—*Jus Canonicum Nova Methodo Explicatum* (5 vols. in 3, Dilingae, 1722), lib. I, tit. 11, n. 83; cf. Reiffenstuel (1641-1703), *Jus Canonicum Universum* (5 vols. in 7, Parisiis, 1864-1870), lib. I, tit. 11, n. 143; Schmalzgrueber (1663-1735) said that it was certain that more than one, or even all minor orders could be conferred on the same day, at least by custom—*Jus Ecclesiasticum Universum* (5 vols. in 12, Romae, 1843-1845), lib. I, tit. 11, nn. 12, 15; Devoti (1744-1820) maintained that the Council of Trent clearly declared, even as to minor orders, that the interstices were to be observed, since it prescribed that they be conferred with the observance of the interstices. Although it specified no definite time interval between the orders, but left this to the judgment of the Bishop, yet its decree should not be so broadly understood that the intervals should be dispensed even without a just cause—*Institutionum Canonicarum Libri IV* (2 vols., Gandae, 1836), lib. I, tit. IV, nn. 4, 5. Many (✠ 1922) said: "Inter primam tonsuram et ostiariatum, nulla requiritur interstitia: nihil enim hac de re statuit conc. Trid., nec ulla alia lex

Gasparri (1852-1934), therefore, held that anyone who taught that no interstices were prescribed for the reception of minor orders was in error. He stated that the interval in conformity with the mind of the Council of Trent was that in which some increase of doctrine, age and merit between one ordination and the next in minor orders could be noted.[10]

Many felt that if the ordination was not a general one, an interval from one Sunday or feast day to the next sufficed.[11]

Barbosa (1589-1649) was much broader and more liberal in his interpretation. Understanding the law strictly, he allowed all minor orders to be conferred on the same day even without a custom to warrant it, but he tempered this by adding that it was much more proper if this was done only out of necessity or for some other urgent cause.[12]

Nevertheless, on account of the admonition of the Council of Trent that the candidate be promoted gradually, he suggested that some interval be observed, for example, from one feast day to the next, or more safely, from one general ordination to the next. However, he maintained that it was left to the prudence of the Bishop to decide whether all the minor orders were to be conferred together or separately.

---

canonica. Unde eodem die conferri possunt." He said later in the same number, however, that this should not be done without a just cause—*Praelectiones de Sacra Ordinatione* (Parisiis, 1905), n. 108. Pallottini cited a decree of the Sacred Congregation of the Council declaring that a Bishop may confer all minor orders on the same day without observing the interstices if he should judge it expedient—*Collectio Omnium Conclusionum et Resolutionum Quae in causis propositis apud Sacram Congregationem Cardinalium S. Concilii Tridentini Interpretum Prodierunt ab eius institutione anno MDLXIV ad annum MDCCCLX, distinctis titulis alphabetico ordine per materias digesta* (18 vols., Romae, 1868-1895), s. v. "Sacramentum Ordinis," V, n. 9 (in *Lauden.*, 27 apr. 1591). (Hereafter, all the above works cited in this footnote will be cited by the author's name except Many's work, which will be cited Many, *De Sacra Ordin.*)

[10] Gasparri, *Tractatus Canonicus de Sacra Ordinatione* (2 vols., Parisiis-Lugduni, 1893), I, n. 502. (Hereafter cited as Gasparri, *De Sacra Ordin.*)

[11] Many, *De Sacra Ordin.*, n. 108.

[12] *Pastoralis Sollicitudinis, sive De Officio et Potestate Episcopi tripartita descriptio* (Lugduni, 1656), pars II, alleg. XI, nn. 17, 18, 19, 20. (Hereafter cited as Barbosa.)

Indeed, after giving the reason for the observance of the interstices, and even stating that the interstices for minor orders were to be enforced, it does not seem plausible that the Council would have tolerated a simultaneous conferring of minor orders without a just cause. Some interval was definitely intended.

Moreover, if the circumstances of the period are considered, there seems to be no doubt that a systematic interval in the conferring of all orders was contemplated by the Fathers. As is known, ecclesiastical discipline had relaxed and a new arrangement for the preparation of the ministers of the Church was sought. Certainly, there would be no benefit to the candidate for the priesthood if he were not impressed with the significance of each new step leading to its attainment. The purpose of the law would indeed have been frustrated if there had not been intended some period of time for consideration of the importance of the duties imposed, or if no duration of time had been contemplated for furnishing an occasion of meditation on the newly acquired grace.

In the constitutions of the Provincial Council of Naples convoked in the year 1699, Ordinaries were given a grave warning relative to the results of an imprudent dispensation from the interstices.[13]

B. Interstices between Minor Orders and Subdiaconate, and between the Major Orders

The intervals between the orders of acolyte and subdeacon, and also between the various major orders were treated specifically by the Council. The lapse of a full year after the conferring of these orders was required before the candidate could be promoted to the next order.[14]

Gasparri declared that the reason for the determination of a year was that it was expedient that the candidate's divine vocation

---

[13] "Sancta Synodus Ordinarios in Domino obsecrat, ut interstitiorum observantiam negligi non patiantur . . . ne ii forte semper esse desinant, quod immature esse festinant."—*Coll. Lac.*, I, 190, n. 12.

[14] Conc. Trident., sess. XXIII, *de ref.*, c. 11, 13, 14; Pallottini, s. v. "Sacramentum Ordinis," V, n. 26 (in *Cervien. Ordinationis*, 16 nov. 1652).

and probity of life be tested by more mature understanding and experience before these sacred ordinations.[15]

The Fathers felt the need of being more definite in regard to the period of probation preceding the conferring of sacred orders, and tried to avoid any occasion for dubious interpretation. They knew if they were not clear, candidates would seek opportunities for accelerated promotion, and this undue haste would result in the ordination of ministers with untested appreciation for the greatness of the gift received. There could be permitted no risk of the inordinate reception of orders, and of a consequent failure of appreciation of their full value.

C. *Special Legislation as to the Conferring of Two Sacred Orders on the Same Day*

The Council of Trent expressly decreed that two sacred orders shall not be conferred on the same day. The legislation included regulars among those bound, all privileges and indults to the contrary notwithstanding.[16]

There was no faculty given by the Council of Trent to anyone to promote or dispense in order that one might receive two sacred orders on one day. Consequently, even if the Metropolitan ordered a Bishop to do so, the Bishop was bound to disregard the mandate, because the Bishop or the Metropolitan or any other person inferior to the Pope could not dispense from the canons unless the faculty was given to them. Obeying the mandate of the Metropolitan did not relieve the Bishop of the responsibility,

[15] Gasparri, *De Sacra Ordin.*, n. 503.

[16] Conc. Trident., sess. XXIII, *de ref.*, c. 13; Barbosa, pars. II, alleg. XIV, nn. 5, 10; Gonzalez-Tellez, lib. I, tit. 11, cap. 15, n. 9; Fagnanus, II, *de temporibus ordinationum et qualitate ordinandorum*, cap. *De eo*, n. 1; Pirhing, lib. I, tit. 11, n. 84; Schmalzgrueber, lib. I, tit. 11, n. 15; Reiffenstuel, lib. I, tit. 11, n. 161; Gasparri, *De Sacra Ordin.*, I, n. 508; Wernz (1842-1914), *Ius Decretalium* (2. ed., 6 vols., Romae-Prati, 1906-1913), II, n. 70 (Hereafter cited, Wernz, *Ius Decretalium*); Many, *De Sacra Ordin.*, nn. 113, 169; S.C.C., *Nullius*, 18 sept. 1597, ad 3—*Codicis Iuris Canonici Fontes cura Emi Petri Card. Gasparri editi* (9 vols., Romae [postea Civitate Vaticana]: Typis Polyglottis Vaticanis, 1923-1939. Vols. VII-IX ed. cura et studio Emi Iustiniani Card. Serédi), n. 2320. (Hereafter cited, *Fontes*.)

and he was liable for any punishment incurred for violating this law.[17]

If the mandate of the Metropolitan, however, was contrary to a law from which he could dispense, such as the reduction of the intervals between sacred orders, he was to be obeyed because he tacitly or *ipso facto* dispensed.[18]

The Holy Father alone could promote to two sacred orders on the same day, or grant a dispensation that others might do so. The decree was one of positive law which did not oblige the Pope, and he could also release others from its obligation.[19]

An interesting case regarding this legislation is recorded in the Decretals.[20] A Bishop conferred diaconate Saturday evening, and on Sunday morning ordained the cleric to the priesthood. The situation was brought to the attention of Pope Innocent III (1201) who forthwith ordered an investigation.

The rule on the conferring of orders forbade ordinations to sacred orders on Sunday, and the conferring of two sacred orders on Saturday, the only day on which sacred ordination was permitted.[21] The Bishop alleged that by the continuation of the fast, either Saturday was prolonged to Sunday, or Sunday was merged with Saturday, so that the interval, if one may be imagined, was neither part of Saturday nor a portion of Sunday, but formed, as it were, an interval not contemplated in the ordinary reckoning of time.[22]

This constituted a canonical fiction, namely, that the union of Saturday evening and Sunday morning made one day. The Pon-

[17] Pirhing, lib. I, tit. 11, n. 87; Fagnanus, II, *de temporibus ordinationum et qualitate ordinandorum*, cap. *Litteras*, n. 1, cap. *Dilectus*, nn. 1, 2; Reiffenstuel, lib. I, tit. 11, n. 162; Many, *De Sacra Ordin.*, n. 113.

[18] Pirhing, *loc. cit.*

[19] Barbosa, pars. II, alleg. XVIII, n. 1 and alleg. L, n. 17; Fagnanus, II, *de temporibus ordinationum et qualitate ordinandorum*, cap. *De eo*, n. 19; Schmalzgrueber, lib. I, tit. 11, n. 9; Gasparri, *De Sacra Ordin.*, I, n. 508.

[20] C. 13, X, *de temporibus ordinationum et qualitate ordinandorum*, I, 11—A. Potthast, *Regesta Pontificum Romanorum inde ab anno post Christum natum MCXCVIII ad annum MCCIV* (2 vols., Berolini, 1874-1875).

[21] C. 1, 2, 3, X, *de temporibus ordinationum et qualitate ordinandorum*, I, 11—Jaffé, nn. 13, 769; 13, 948.

[22] "Continuatio de duobus facit unum."—*Glossa Ordinaria*, ad c. 13, X, *de temporibus ordinationum et qualitate ordinandorum*, I, 11, s. v. *continuationem*.

tiff pointed out that if it was not lawful for a Bishop to confer two sacred orders on the same day, by the same reason it was not lawful to confer one order on one day and another on the next with a continuation of the fast, since by continuing the fast in order to create a canonical fiction, either Sunday morning was carried back to Saturday, or Saturday evening was carried over to Sunday, thus constituting one day. But, he continued, if one should say that Sunday morning pertains to one day and Saturday evening to another, the Bishop's action was still without justification because, as Alexander III had decreed, only the Pope could confer sacred orders on Sunday,[23] and the Bishop would have been ordaining to the priesthood on Sunday. Furthermore, if the Bishop persisted in his argument, maintaining that the combining of Saturday evening and Sunday morning made another day, an eighth day of the week as it were, his conduct was still contrary to the law because he could not offer two Masses the same day.[24]

Therefore, because of this *inordinata ordinatio,* as Pope Innocent III referred to it, the Pope suspended the Bishop from conferring the orders of diaconate and priesthood, and the ordained was forbidden to exercise the office of the priesthood until dispensed, according to the rule expressed in the gloss: *quis debet puniri in eo in quo deliquit.*

The glossator explained the justice of the sentence. The ordaining Prelate was suspended from conferring the orders of diaconate and priesthood, and the ordained from the exercise of the order of priesthood only. The reason given by the glossator is that the Bishop by his office should be more prudent, and hence erred more grievously.

Gonzalez-Tellez (✠ ca. 1674) explained how the practice of ordination in the evening was justified. He stated that this was not without precedent in the Church, since the first ordination, namely that of the Apostles, was held in the evening.[25] Accordingly, because of the example of Christ, it was customary and

---

[23] C. 1, X, *de temporibus ordinationum et qualitate ordinandorum,* I, 11—Jaffé, n. 13, 769.

[24] C. 3, X, *de celebratione Missarum et sacramento Eucharistiae, et divinis officiis,* III, 41—Potthast, n. 2668.

[25] Luke, xxii, 14-21; Gonzalez-Tellez, lib. I, tit. 11, cap. 15, n. 4.

even fitting that ordinations be held at that hour. The introduction of this custom was also indirectly the result of the persecutions suffered by the Christians in the first centuries, on account of which they could not easily congregate except at late hours.[26]

Pirhing (1606-1679) alleged that a general ordination, even to major orders, begun on Saturday could be finished on Sunday morning, if on account of the large number of ordinands, or for some other reasonable cause, it could not be completed Saturday. Accordingly, by a canonical fiction Sunday morning was to be considered a part of Saturday because of the continuation of the Ember fast. As was seen above, sacred orders could be conferred only on Saturday. Of course, Pirhing required that the natural fast be continued both by the ordaining Bishop and the ordinands. He also restricted this procedure to the ordination of those only who did not receive a sacred order on Saturday, because if those who did receive a sacred order on Saturday were to receive another on Sunday morning, by a canonical fiction they would have received two sacred orders in one day, and this was forbidden whether the day was a true and natural day or a fictitious one.[27]

D. Lack of Prescribed Interval between the Priesthood and the Episcopate

There is no prescribed interval required by the Council of Trent between the ordination to the priesthood and the consecration to the Episcopate. The Council simply said that the person who was to be promoted had to be constituted at least six months previously in sacred orders.[28] Gasparri contended that this meant that six months must elapse not from the ordination to any sacred

---

[26] Gonzalez-Tellez, *loc. cit.*

[27] Pirhing, lib. I, tit. 11, nn. 84, 85; Gonzalez-Tellez, lib. I, tit. 11, cap. 13, n. 3; Barbosa, pars. II, alleg. XVIII, n. 1; Fagnanus, II, *de temporibus ordinationum et qualitate ordinandorum,* cap. *De eo,* n. 18; Reiffenstuel, lib. I, tit. 11, n. 163; Schmalzgrueber, lib. I, tit. 11, n. 16; S.C.C., *Nullius,* 18 sept. 1597, ad 3—*Fontes,* n. 2320.

[28] "Everyone who is hereafter to be promoted to a cathedral church . . . shall also for the space of at least six months previously have been constituted in sacred orders."—Conc. Trident., sess. XXIII, *de ref.,* c. 2; Schroeder, p. 153.

order, but from the ordination to the priesthood.[29] Barbosa, Pirhing, Reiffenstuel, Schmalzgrueber, Wernz, and Many maintained that this referred to the first reception of sacred orders as the point from which computation was required. This meant that after six months from the ordination to the subdiaconate the cleric could be promoted to the episcopate.[30] These authors affirmed that one could not argue from the Constitution of Gregory XIV, issued in 1591,[31] that this decree of the Council of Trent denoted six months from the ordination to the priesthood, as Gasparri inferred,[32] since the Constitution did nothing more than restate the decree of the Council of Trent.[33] Therefore they argued, there was no reason on account of which a deacon who was ordained a priest on Saturday could not be consecrated a Bishop on the following Sunday.[34]

Many claimed that a priest could not be consecrated a Bishop on the same day, because this would violate the decree of the Council of Trent which prohibited the conferring of two sacred orders on one and the same day.[35] The opposite opinion was held by Pirhing, Reiffenstuel and Schmalzgrueber.[36] Two reasons were given for the latter view: first, the laws and canons which prescribed the interstices were to be understood of those orders only which were conferred at ordinary and general ordinations, and the episcopate was an extraordinary ordination; secondly, the episcopate was really only a culmination of the priesthood, and thus the two were only inadequately distinguished.

---

[29] Gasparri, *De Sacra Ordin.*, I, n. 514.

[30] Barbosa, pars. II, alleg. I, n. 36; Pirhing, lib. I, tit. 11, n. 85; Reiffenstuel, lib. I, tit. 11, n. 165; Schmalzgrueber, lib. I, tit. 11, n. 16; Wernz, *Ius Decretalium,* II, n. 70; Many, *De Sacra Ordin.*, n. 108.

[31] Gregorius XIV, const. *Onus,* 15 maii 1591—*Bullarum Diplomatum et Privilegiorum Sanctorum Romanorum Pontificum Taurinensis Editio* (25 vols., Augustae Taurinorum, 1857-1872), IX, 419. (Hereafter cited as *Bull. Rom. Taur.*)

[32] Gasparri, *loc. cit.*

[33] Wernz, *loc. cit.;* Many, *loc. cit.*

[34] Many, *loc. cit.*

[35] Many, *loc. cit.*

[36] Pirhing, *loc. cit.;* Reiffenstuel, *loc. cit.;* Schmalzgrueber, *loc. cit.*

ARTICLE 3. DISPENSATIONS

Concerning the intervals for minor orders, the Council stated simply that the interstices were to be observed unless the Bishop should deem it more expedient to act otherwise.[37]

As to the interstices between the order of an acolyte and the order of a subdeacon, the Council did not wish to make the interval of a year so stringent that nobody could dispense from it under any circumstances. The year was to be observed unless necessity *or* the need of the Church should in the judgment of the Bishop require otherwise.[38]

No aspirant was to be promoted to the diaconate until he had completed a year in the order of the subdiaconate, unless the Bishop should judge otherwise.[39]

The candidate was to be ordained to the priesthood only after he had served a year in the order of the diaconate, unless by reason of the advantage *and* need of the Church, the Bishop should judge otherwise.[40]

To dispense from the required interval between the order of an acolyte and the order of a subdeacon, the necessity of *or* the utility for the Church was a prerequisite to warrant the dispensation. Necessity or utility was not required to dispense from the required interval of a year between the subdiaconate and the diaconate, but the Bishop was bound to have a just cause for action in order to justify the dispensation; but, both utility *and* necessity were demanded to make lawful any dispensation from the time which was to elapse between the diaconate and the priesthood.

It is true that the interstices were never essential for the valid reception of orders, but certainly their observance was necessary for the lawful reception of orders.[41]

---

[37] Conc. Trident., sess. XXIII, *de ref.*, c. 11.

[38] Conc. Trident., sess. XXIII, *de ref.*, c. 11.

[39] Conc. Trident., sess. XXIII, *de ref.*, c. 13.

[40] Conc. Trident., sess. XXIII, *de ref.*, c. 14.

[41] "Interstitium est de lege positiva et non de substantia ordinis."—Fagnanus, II, *de temporibus ordinationum et qualitate ordinandorum*, cap. *De eo*, n. 20.

A. Causes for Dispensing from the Interstices Required for the Conferring of Minor Orders and Diaconate

Reiffenstuel, Barbosa, and Schmalzgrueber advanced the opinion that any cause, even thought it was not one of necessity, sufficed to dispense from the interstices for minor orders. According to their view, all that the Council of Trent required of the Bishop was that he judge it expedient in this or that case. Reiffenstuel (1641-1703) cited the approved custom in many places of conferring all the minor orders on the same day and in the same ordination, since this manner of proceeding seemed more desirable to the Bishops in the larger dioceses.[42]

In regard to the interstices between the subdiaconate and the diaconate, Gasparri (1852-1934) said the Bishop had power to dispense even though the necessity of or the usefulness for the Church was not present as a reason. However, he insisted that even for this dispensation a just cause was required at the judgment of the Bishop, and, in general, a graver cause was required for a dispensation affecting the interval between the subdiaconate and the diaconate than for one affecting the interval between the various minor orders themselves. The decision of the justice or the sufficiency of the cause, however, was left to the will and prudence of the Bishop, e.g. that the ordinand had to be away from the diocese for studies was a sufficient cause for dispensing from the interstices for the diaconate if he could not otherwise be present at the general ordination.[43]

B. A Major Cause is Required to Dispense from the Interval between Minor Orders and Subdiaconate, and from That between Diaconate and Priesthood

The cause warranting a dispensation from the interstices between the subdiaconate and the diaconate did not need to be as great as the reason required for dispensing from the interval between minor orders and subdiaconate. This was evident from the

[42] Reiffenstuel, lib. I, tit. 11, n. 148; Barbosa, pars. II, alleg. XVIII, n. 4; Schmalzgrueber, lib. I, tit. 11, n. 14.

[43] Gasparri, *De Sacra Ordin.*, I, n. 505; Reiffenstuel, lib. I, tit. 11, n. 149.

canon of the Council of Trent where the dispensing from the former interval was left to the judgment of the Bishop, while the dispensing from the latter interval was made dependent on the necessity of or the utility for the Church. The reason was that in a promotion from the subdiaconate to the diaconate no new change of state was obtained; in the transition from minor orders to subdiaconate, the state of life of the cleric was changed, inasmuch as he was precluded from returning to secular pursuits and from entrance upon a conjugal life. Consequently, it seemed reasonable that the subdiaconate should be received with greater previous opportunity for calm consideration, and that the indicated interval should be properly sustained and not dispensed except with greater reason than might be required in other stages of advancement in the clerical ranks.[44]

According to the decrees of the Council of Trent, it seems that a greater cause was required for dispensing from the interval between the diaconate and the priesthood,[45] than that decreed as requisite for a dispensation from the interval between minor orders and subdiaconate.[46]

Reiffenstuel said that the interval between the diaconate and the priesthood had to be observed above all because of the excellence of the order of the priesthood and the imminence of the active ministry, and accordingly a longer preparation was needed unless the Bishop should judge otherwise according to law. Besides, according to the wording of the Council of Trent, as to the

[44] Reiffenstuel, lib. I, tit. 11, n. 149; "Quia ministerium diaconatus his temporibus minori indiget probatione, cum jam in desuetudinem abierint canonicae leges in quibus multa diaconis committebantur quae valde exactam personae cujus fidei tradenda erant cognitionem et experientiam requirebant; et alias diaconatus nullam addit de novo obligationem aut vinculum sive castitatis servandae, sive officii divini recitandi, quod non trahit secum subdiaconatus."—Honorante, *Praxis Secretariae Tribunalis Cardinalis Urbis Vicarii* (2. ed., Romae, 1762), cap. IV, n. 1 (hereafter cited Honorante); Many, *De Sacra Ordin.*, n. 108.

[45] ". . . unless by reason of the advantage *and* need of the Church the Bishop should judge otherwise. . . ."—Conc. Trident., sess. XXIII, *de ref.*, c. 14; Schroeder, p. 173.

[46] ". . . unless necessity *or* the utility of the Church shall in the judgment of the Bishop require otherwise."—Conc. Trident., sess. XXIII, *de ref.*, c. 11; Schroeder, p. 171.

interval between minor orders and subdiaconate, necessity *or* utility sufficed for dispensing, while for the interval between the diaconate and the priesthood, both necessity *and* utility simultaneously had to be present to justify the dispensation. Therefore, it is manifest that a cause of greater significance should be present in the latter case. In the former the causes were to be understood disjunctively, while in the latter case, they were to be taken conjunctively.[47] Barbosa,[48] Pirhing[49] and Many[50] agreed with Reiffenstuel's assertion.

A decree of the Provincial Council of Benevento (1693) also supported this view.[51]

A more liberal view was adopted by Gasparri. He maintained that in the intervals both between the order of an acolyte and the order of a subdeacon, and also between the diaconate and the priesthood, the Bishop could dispense either because of the necessity of or the utility for the Church, that is, whenever necessity or usefulness to the Church required this accelerated promotion. According to this opinion, the Bishop could dispense from the interval before the priesthood, for example, on the sole score of usefulness.[52]

---

[47] Reiffenstuel, lib. I, tit. 11, nn. 149, 150.

[48] Barbosa, pars. II, alleg. XVIII, n. 4.

[49] Pirhing, lib. I, tit. 11, n. 91.

[50] Many, *De Sacra Ordin.*, n. 108.

[51] Tit. V, cap. 3: "Quia vero ii promovendi sunt, qui pie et fideliter in ministeriis anteactis se gesserant, ad hoc dignoscendum temporum interstitia sancita sunt. Caveant igitur Episcopi, ne super hujusmodi interstitiis dispensare audeant, nisi causa, quae est Ecclesiae necessitas vel utilitas, prius cognita et diligenter perpensa, praesertim si de interstitiis a Diaconatu ad Presbyteratum agatur, ad quae dispensanda necessitas *simul et* utilitas Ecclesiae requiruntur. . . ."—*Coll. Lac.*, I, 28, b.

[52] Gasparri, *De Sacra Ordin.*, I, n. 504.

CHAPTER III

The Law of Interstices in the Present Code

Article 1. As to Tonsure and Minor Orders

The Council of Trent did not legislate in regard to an interval between first tonsure[1] and minor orders, but it did prescribe that the four minor orders be conferred at intervals, unless it appeared more expedient to the Bishop to act otherwise. Hence, according to the Tridentine legislation, tonsure and the four minor orders, or even the four minor orders with the accompanying first tonsure, could not be conferred on the same day. The latitude of the legislation gave rise to various local customs. In the city of Rome, Innocent XI on February 20, 1673, ordained that tonsure should not be conferred in the future with the four minor orders, but only with the first two. Benedict XIII on May 20, 1725, decreed that tonsure be given alone without any minor order, and the custom thenceforth obtained of conferring tonsure separately, then the first two minor orders, and later the second two minor orders.[2] The Roman custom is suggested now by the common law, and extended to the Universal Church.[3]

The first paragraph of canon 978 on interstices in the Code of Canon Law does not prescribe or even suggest intervals, but leaves them to the prudent judgment of the Bishop. However, in order to insure at least two intervals, the Code declares in the third paragraph of the same canon that it is not lawful to confer tonsure and one of the minor orders, or all the minor orders collectively on a candidate simultaneously.

---

[1] "Dicitur prima quia, ut constanter feratur, opus est repetitis tonsuris, quae tamen, privatim factae, effectum initiationis non pariunt."—Vermeersch-Creusen, *Epitome Iuris Canonici* (Vol. II, 5. ed., Mechliniae-Romae: H. Dessain, 1934), II, n. 236. (Cited hereafter as Vermeersch-Creusen, *Epitome.*)

[2] Honorante, cap. I, n. 6.

[3] Can. 978, § 3.

Three separate ordinations are thus contemplated by canon 978, since not only must tonsure be conferred separately, but also the minor orders themselves cannot be conferred conjointly. This disjunction of orders, however, does not solve the problem of what intervals are intended, but rather recommends what groups the ordinations are to occupy.[4]

That there is justification in referring to the conferring of tonsure as an ordination is vouched for in the text of canon 950.[5] Tonsure, admittedly, is not an order, but the process whereby tonsure is given can be referred to as a true ordination.[6]

Thus the ordinations inferior to major orders are divided distinctly into two groups: tonsure and minor orders. Tonsure absolutely stands alone in law as a separate ceremony. Minor orders, however, must be conferred at two separate intervals which necessitates a division into two ordination ceremonies of the acts through which the orders are conferred. There is no prohibitory clause in the law of the Code to forbid the conferring of two orders at each ordination, or even of three at the first and of one at the second, or the reception of one order at the first ceremony and the latter three minor orders at the second.[7] That much latitude certainly is allowed by the canon on interstices. Accordingly, it is left to the decision of the Bishop as to which plan he wishes to adopt. The arrangement in Rome as stated above when reference was made to the evolution of the manner in the conferring of the ordinations under Innocent XI and Benedict XIII is in general use.[8]

---

[4] Blat, *Commentarium Textus Codicis Iuris Canonici* (5 vols. in 6, Romae: F. Ferrari, 1921-1927), III, pars. I, 329. (Cited hereafter as Blat, *Commentarium.)*

[5] Canon 950: "In iure verba: *ordinare, ordo, ordinatio, sacra ordinatio,* comprehundunt, praeter consecrationem episcopalem, ordines enumeratos in can. 949 et ipsam primam tonsuram. . . ."

[6] "Prima autem tonsura cum nullam conferat potestatem, non est sacramentum, sed initiatio ad statum clericalem, quo clerici a laicis distinguuntur. Ecclesia tamen, in eius collatione vult ut normae de sacramentis conferendis observentur: ac proin verba 'ordinare, ordo, ordinatio' comprehundunt . . . ipsam tonsuram."—Vermeersch-Creusen, *Epitome,* II, n. 236.

[7] Noldin (1838-1922), *Summa Theologiae Moralis* (25. ed., recognita ab A. Schmitt, 3 vols., Oeniponte: Felician Rauch, 1938), III, n. 477.

[8] Cf. *supra,* p. 26.

The Roman method of conferring tonsure first, then the orders of porter and lector, and finally those of exorcist and acolyte appears as the most logical and balanced order, and the fact that it is so generally adopted adds strength to the assertion. Obviously; there would usually be no reason for having five separate ordinations, though in fact that many could be contemplated under the provision of canon 978, § 1. Such an extension would possibly be in order in a diocese where ordinations are infrequent, in order to impress the people with the sacredness and the symbolism of the rites, or where an effort is being made to foster vocations when there is a deficiency of native priests.

On the other hand, however, the arrangement as current in Rome and in the Church at large does not impose too great a burden on the candidate. This system fulfills the object of the interstices adequately, namely, to allow him an opportunity to prepare for each order, and at the same time sufficiently to impress him with the significance of the order received. However, one must not lose sight of the possibility of the conferring of three minor orders at the first ordination and of one minor order at the second, or of one minor order at the first ordination and of three at the second. If any criticism arises, it would come from the fact that the universal practice is not followed rather than that the law is contravened, and it could therefore be disregarded.

The Council of Trent was not so definite in stating the number of ordinations, and merely decreed the observance of the prescribed interstices.[9] Whether or not the interstices adopted by the Council of Trent were to become actualized according to the prescription of the individual Bishop is undecided. The Code, however, is just as indefinite as to the actual time which is required to elapse between the ordinations to minor orders. The law in this respect seems content to permit the commentator to seek dates from other parts of the Code, namely, from canons dealing with the times of ordination, the retreats scheduled, the required course of studies, the age of the ordinand, etc. Authors commenting on this canon do not specify or even suggest fixed intervals. However, if the interstices are adapted to the days of ordinations, definite intervals can then be established for tonsure

[9] Conc. Trident., sess. XXIII, *de ref.*, c. 11; Schroeder, p. 171.

and minor orders. The legislation appointing the times for ordinations states that tonsure may be conferred on any day at any hour.[10] This will allow much freedom to the Bishop in arranging the call for the conferring of tonsure. In other words, he can approximate the time of ordination to the first tonsure to the time of ordination to the first minor order as closely as the day before the latter is scheduled. Thus, if there is need, he can also delay the conferring of tonsure until the fitness of the aspirant is more favorably ascertained, if there is doubt as to the sincerity and worthiness of the candidate. Because of the significance of tonsure as the first step to the priesthood, this margin is most acceptable because, as the Code states, first tonsure shall be conferred only on those who have the intention of advancing to the priesthood, and of whom one may reasonably expect that they will be worthy priests.[11]

Minor orders may be conferred on Sundays and feasts which are doubles, but in the forenoon of the day.[12] Again the Code is most generous in providing for a suitable ordination date. Cappello asserts that the Bishop may, in accordance with the rule stated in canon 1006, § 4, confer minor orders on any feast greater than a simple or a semi-double feast.[13]

From the concession of paragraph 4 of canon 1006, the burden of when to call the aspirant to orders rests solidly with the Bishop's judgment, because the Bishop may ordain to minor orders on any day during the greater part of the year, since by far the feasts greater than a semi-double are in the majority. Of course, the Bishop could not omit an order, or vary the sequence, for orders must be conferred in their proper succession, so that the omission of any intermediate order is absolutely forbidden.[14]

---

[10] Canon 1006, § 4: "Prima tonsura quolibet die et hora conferri potest. . . ."

[11] Canon 973, § 1; Vermeersch-Creusen, *Epitome,* II, n. 244; Beste, *Introductio in Codicem* (Collegeville, Minnesota: St. John's Abbey Press, 1938), p. 518.

[12] Canon 1006, § 4: ". . . ordines minores singulis diebus dominicis et festis duplicibus, mane tamen."

[13] Cappello, *Tractatus Canonico—Moralis de Sacramentis,* Vol. II, Pars III, *De Sacra Ordinatione* (Romae: Marietti, 1935), n. 565. (Hereafter cited *Tractatus de Sacramentis.)*

[14] Canon 977.

In a private response given January 20, 1941, the Sacred Congregation of the Sacraments replied that the ordinations referred to in canon 1006, § 2, 3, are general ordinations, and consequently whenever they may be performed, first tonsure and minor orders may also be conferred, although there be no ordination to sacred orders.[15] Even before this reply, Vermeersch-Creusen maintained that this inclusion was clearly in the mind of the legislator, and also that such was the practice in Rome.[16]

The Bishop must be careful in his schedule of ordinations, so that the last and highest minor order, that of the acolyte, is not conferred within less than a year of the appointed ordination to the first major order, the subdiaconate.[17]

There will be no attempt here to determine a model set of interstices for observance in the conferring of tonsure and the minor orders. There are too many conditions to weigh which would result in hardship if a certain application were forced on each diocese. Circumstances vary in each case, and the Code seems to have taken care of any necessity. All that the Bishop is to determine is whether the purpose of the interstices, i.e., the significance of the orders conferred, has been established in the candidate and whether the latter is worthy; after that he is free to ordain whenever he wishes, if all other temporal conditions are verified, such as the required age, the set course of studies, etc. Generally Bishops leave the judgment as to worthiness and preparation to the seminary faculties, but the Bishop must not lose sight of the fact that he is primarily responsible, for it is he who calls the candidate to orders. Under normal circumstances Bishops are also content to let the seminary authorities determine the ordination date, since they are in a better position through close contact with the candidate to ascertain his mental, moral, and physical qualities, in accordance with which the apt times for ordination are to be fixed. However, in law the Bishop may determine the date himself, so that if circumstances arise in view of which a candidate must receive tonsure and minor orders in a

---

[15] S. C. de Sacr., January 20, 1941 (Private) as reported in Bouscaren, *The Canon Law Digest* (2 vols., Milwaukee: The Bruce Publishing Co., 1934-1943), II, 250.

[16] *Epitome,* II, n. 269.

[17] Canon 978, § 2.

short space of time, the Bishop may feel free to compress the period accordingly.

ARTICLE 2. AS TO THE SUBDIACONATE

Once the candidate has received tonsure and the minor orders, the interstices become definite under normal conditions, i. e. those in which no dispensation is in order. Perhaps the sacredness of the steps about to be taken necessitates greater circumspection and a more precise specification of the preparatory periods of time. Furthermore, one must remember that in receiving successive major orders the candidate is approaching ever closer to what may be called the active ministry. As regards tonsure and the minor orders, a remote participation in the order of priesthood may, indeed, be recognized under each advance, but one must observe that the duties conferred by these various orders are more symbolic than active, insofar as they actually devolve for the greater part either upon lay people or upon the higher ministers of the Church.

The Code requires an interval of one year between the reception of the order of an acolyte and the order of a subdeacon.[18] The terminus *a quo* is not fixed, since the date for the conferring of the order of acolyte is not definitely determined. The computation of the year is not a maximum but a minimum. Accordingly, it is not necessary to fix the year exactly, but any time after the lapse of a year is lawful for the ordination to the diaconate. Again, the Code gives an ample selection of ordination dates for sacred orders. It decrees that major orders are to be conferred during Mass on the Ember Saturdays, on the Saturday before Passion Sunday, and on Holy Saturday, but for a grave reason the Bishop may have these ordinations also on any Sunday or holyday of obligation.[19]

---

[18] Canon 978, § 2: ". . . acolythus vero ad subdiaconatum . . . ne antea promoveatur, quam acolythus unum saltem annum . . . in suo quisque ordine fuerit versatus, nisi necessitas aut utilitas Ecclesiae, iudicio Episcopi, aliud exposcat."

[19] Canon 1006, § 2, 3: "Ordinationes in sacris celebrentur intra Missarum sollemnia sabbatis Quatuor Temporum, sabbato ante dominicam Passionis, et Sabbato Sancto;"

"Gravi tamen causa interveniente, Episcopus potest eas habere etiam quolibet die dominico aut festo de praecepto."

The Holy See was asked by the Apostolic Delegate of the United States to grant in favor of the Archbishops and Bishops of this country the faculty to have sacred ordinations outside the times fixed by law, namely on feast days of the double rite of the first or second class though not of obligation, and on some Saturdays at the close of the scholastic year. In an audience of May 18, 1940, Pope Pius XII, having heard the report of the Prefect of the Sacred Congregation of the Sacraments, and in view of the representations of the Most Reverend Apostolic Delegate, deigned to grant to the aforesaid Archbishops and Bishops the faculty petitioned, for three years, subject to the observance of the provisions of law.[20]

It is pertinent here to establish the meaning of *holyday of obligation,* for to know the extent of the application of the term will help to determine the scope of possible ordination dates. A doubt may arise whether the term *holyday of obligation* includes also the suppressed feast days. If it did, it would enlarge considerably the number of possible ordination dates. However, the Pontifical Commission for the Interpretation of the Code replied that the words *festo de praecepto* in canon 1006, § 3, do not include feasts which have been suppressed in the universal Church by the Code.[21]

This solution would leave ten possible dates for the conferring of major orders on holydays of obligation, besides the fifty-two Sundays of the year. A further question may be raised as to whether the term *festo de praecepto* includes all the feasts of obligation, or just those which are in force in the United States. This point was adjusted by a private response of the Most Reverend Apostolic Delegate to the Chancellor of the Diocese of Ogdensburg on May 11, 1938. The question was asked whether according to canon 1006, § 3, major orders could licitly be conferred on the Feast of Corpus Christi which, though a feast of

---

[20] Private response to the Most Reverend Apostolic Delegate of the United States (S. C. de Sacr., 18 maii 1940), as reported in Bouscaren, *The Canon Law Digest,* II, 249.

[21] Pontifical Commission for the Interpretation of the Code, response of May 25, 1936—*Acta Apostolicae Sedis, Commentarium Officiale* (Romae [Civitate Vaticana], 1909-), XXVIII (1936), 210 (Hereafter cited as *AAS);* reported also in Bouscaren, *The Canon Law Digest,* II, 248.

obligation by the general law,[22] is not such in the United States, being transferred by indult to the following Sunday. The reply stated that it is for the Ordinary to decide whether the circumstances constitute a sufficiently grave cause to permit ordination to the priesthood on the Feast of Corpus Christi. If the decision of the Ordinary is in the affirmative, then there is no reason why he may not follow the opinion that canon 1006, § 3 includes holydays which are by the Code in force everywhere, although there is a dispensation from their obligation in the place of ordination.[23]

In order to establish a clear concept of the elements involved in the discussion of the year, it is necessary to fix the identities of this term, as regarded under different considerations. The account of the different modes of reckoning the year can be considered complete for the immediate purpose here with a definition of the *moral* and the *physical* computation of the year. *Moral* is a more elastic term than *physical.* The *moral* computation of time is meant when one speaks of "about a year's time," or "nearly a year's time." In short, it gives much latitude to those who are obliged to act under a law which allows the *moral* interpretation of time. Thus, in present day terminology, the word *moral,* as applied to time reckoning, simply signifies a more or less accurate computation which at least approximates the reality of the truly physical reckoning of time. Accordingly, a *moral* interpretation or determination of midnight, for example, would allow one, when fasting from midnight, to take food even ten or fifteen minutes after the moment which fixes midnight according to any of the physical standards indicated in canon 33, § 1. However, there is no reference here to the Eucharistic fast from midnight for which a *physical* computation is required.[24]

The calculation of time, on the other hand, is said to be *physical* when the computation is definite and exact. There is no room

---

[22] Canon 1247, § 1.

[23] Letter of the Most Reverend Apostolic Delegate of the United States, dated May 13, 1938, as reported in Bouscaren, *The Canon Law Digest,* II, 248-249.

[24] Dubé, *The General Principles for the Reckoning of Time in Canon Law,* The Catholic University of America Canon Law Studies, n. 144 (Washington, D. C.: The Catholic University of America Press, 1941), p. 88.

in considering time in this sense for the words "about" or "nearly," since the time must be clearly and precisely determined. Thus, there is no possibility of deviation from the perfectly calculated period, no opportunity for an interpretation that would permit nearness to the exact time as sufficient to be within the compass of the computation required. In the computation of time according to this method there is no justification for employing the rule, "a very small matter is held as nothing."[25]

The term *moral* can also be understood in another way. For instance, if two courses of reckoning are presented, the more favorable is allowed as a preference. This is especially true in regard to the intervals of ordination. There one is met not only with an interval of time between orders, but also with the legally required day of ordination, or rather the set times of the ordination. As can be readily seen, the way is open for the use of the liturgical calendar, which is drawn up according to feast days whose date is variable from year to year, rather than of the civil calendar, which estimates the year as consisting of 365 days.

The discussion as to which reckoning of the year is understood in canon 978, § 2, justifies this mention of the two calendars. The liturgical or ecclesiastical calendar is constructed on the basis of the repetition of feasts which occur at different times each year. This determination of elapsed time fits suitably under the denomination of a *moral* reckoning. The juridical calendar, on the other hand, is fixed by numbers, e.g., 7 days in a week, 30 days in a month, 365 days in a year.[26] This enumeration, of course, is similar to the civil calendar, although not identical. In the latter one meets the leap year with a total of 366 days in view of variable computation of the month of February as consisting of 29 days rather than of 28 in certain years, according to the period at hand. Furthermore, in the civil calendar, not all the months are of the same duration as in the juridical calendar. The *physical* reckoning is best associated with the civil and juridical calendars.

The method for the computation of the year was undefined by the Council of Trent.[27] However, the consistent and more weighty

---

[25] Cicognani, *Canon Law,* Authorized English Version by O'Hara and Brennan (2. ed., and rev., Philadelphia: Dolphin Press, 1935), p. 682.

[26] Canon 32.

[27] Conc. Trident., sess. XXIII, *de ref.,* c. 11; Schroeder, p. 171.

opinion of the doctors before the Code maintained that the year, as used in the provisions of the Council of Trent, was not conclusively a civil year, but could be understood as meaning also a liturgical year.[28]

Gasparri reasonably maintains that the calculation of the year is to be understood in favor of the ordinand, so that a solar year is not meant if it is of greater duration, but the ecclesiastical year suffices, and vice versa.[29] In support of the same kind of concept, the Sacred Congregation of the Council issued a decree on February 3, 1595, allowing preference of the liturgical year whenever it was shorter.[30]

According to Gasparri's view as expressed above, the year between the reception of the order of acolyte and the order of subdeacon was to be computed by a *moral* reckoning, that is, not necessarily within the scope of 365 days, but as determined by the liturgical calendar from the occurrence of a feast to its repetition the year following. Consequently, a candidate who received the last of the minor orders on Trinity Sunday could be ordained a subdeacon on the corresponding feast of the year following, even though only 340 days had expired as reckoned by the civil calendar. There can be no doubt that a full year has elapsed as the law requires, and since there is no contrary decree forbidding the

---

[28] Barbosa, pars. II, alleg. XVIII, n. 2; Fagnanus, II, *de temporibus ordinationum et qualitate ordinandorum,* cap. *Litteras,* n. 2; Schmalzgrueber, lib. I, tit. 11, n. 12; Pirhing, lib. I, tit. 11, n. 88; Reiffenstuel, lib. I, tit. 11, nn. 144, 145; Pichler (1670-1736), *Epitome Juris Canonici* (2 vols., Venetiis, 1755), lib. I, tit. 11, n. 12; Devoti, lib. I, tit. IV, n. 5; Antonelli (✠ 1694), *Tractatus Novissimus et Absolutissimus de Tempore Legali* (Venetiis: 1692), lib. I, c. III, n. 10; Engel (1634-1674), *Collegium Universi Iuris Canonici* (9. ed., Beneventi: 1760), lib. I, tit. 11, n. 20; Bonacina (1585-1631), *Opera Omnia* (3 vols., Venetiis: 1687), *De Censuris,* disp. III, q. I, punctum IV, § 11, n. 2; Many, *De Sacra Ordin.,* n. 109; Gasparri, *De Sacra Ordin.,* I, n. 503.

[29] Gasparri, *loc. cit.*

[30] The Congregation was asked: "An annus duodecim mensium completus esse debeat, vel sufficiat lapsa esse quatuor interstitia, quae propter varietatem festorum mobilium occurrunt, quousque duodecimus mensis compleatur?". The response was: "Attendendum esse censum quatuor dictorum interstitiorum, non autem tempus duodecim mensium completorum."—S.C.C., 3 febr. 1595, as cited in Wernz, *Ius Decretalium,* II, n. 79.

interpretation of the year that must intervene as a liturgical year, that interpretation may prevail. This is also the observation made by Ayrinhac (1867-1930) and Cappello.[81]

Blat, however, does not favor this opinion and prefers to follow the year as it appears in the civil calendar. He bases his reckoning of the year on canon 34, § 3, 1°, 3°, namely, on the assumption that the months are to be taken according to the civil calendar, and since the starting point does not coincide with the beginning of the day, the first day is not to be counted, and the time expires with the end of the last day of the same date and month in the following year. For example, if a candidate received the order of acolyte on May 25 of one year, he could not, according to the interval required, receive the subdiaconate until May 26 of the year following. This instance, however, does not contemplate the legally specified days of ordination, but serves only as a hypothetical case for illustration.[82]

The point of argument seems to revolve around the use of the word "year." According to canons 31 and 32, the length of the year is 365 days unless the contrary is expressly stipulated. Dubé maintains that the law of interstices is not a liturgical law, and therefore is not excepted from the general norms of time-reckoning as provided in Title III of the First Book of the Code.[83] He concedes that the prescriptions regulating the various intervals to be observed between the reception of orders are closely related to liturgy, but are nevertheless formal disciplinary laws. At most, the law of interstices is a liturgical law in the wide sense, and consequently, since there is no explicit excepting

---

[81] "Between the last minor order, the acolytate, and subdeaconship the Code . . . requires a full year, which may mean a calendar year of 365 or 366 days or a liturgical year; as, for example, from Easter to Easter or from Pentecost to Pentecost; this might in some cases be shorter by several weeks."—Ayrinhac, *Legislation on the Sacraments in the New Code of Canon Law* (New York: Longmans, Green and Co., 1928), n. 296 (Hereafter cited *Legislation on the Sacraments);* Cappello, *Tractatus de Sacramentis,* II, Pars III, n. 419.

[82] Blat, *Commentarium,* III, pars. I, 329.

[83] Canon 31; Dubé, *The General Principles for the Reckoning of Time,* p. 198.

norm provided for the reckoning of these particular intervals, they are to be computed by the general norms of time-reckoning. Moreover, Van Hove declares that only the time-reckoning involved by such liturgical laws as are found in the liturgical books as such is not affected by Title III.[34] Conversely, the computation of time relative to the liturgical laws found in the Code must be made according to canons 32-35; otherwise, there would be no norm with which to reckon the year that must elapse between the reception of the last minor order and the first major order.[35]

Wherefore, the general norms of time-reckoning are to be followed, but the table to be used is not necessarily the civil calendar. In 1941 Holy Saturday fell on April 12, but in 1942 it occurred on April 4. Thus, there is a possibility given of accepting either Holy Saturday in 1941 (according to the liturgical calendar) or April 12 in 1941 (according to the civil calender) as the point of initial reckoning for the year required between the last of the minor orders and the first of the major orders. Since this is a favorable matter, it would seem that either reckoning may be used. Whenever the ecclesiastical year is of a shorter duration, as in the example of Holy Saturday 1941 to Holy Saturday 1942, the ecclesiastical calendar may be followed; and conversely, when the liturgical year is longer, as is the case for the Holy Saturday to Holy Saturday computation for 1942-1943, since in the latter year Holy Saturday occurred on April 24, the civil calendar may be observed, because this is also a juridical calendar under canon 34, § 3, 1°, 3°. The right of a choice between the civil and the liturgical calendar for the reckoning of the required interval of a year appears to be a reasonable interpretation. As long as the law does not seek to destroy an advantage there is also no reason for imposing an unwarranted burden.

---

[34] Van Hove, *Commentarium Lovaniense in Codicem Iuris Canonici,* Vol. I, Tomus III, *De Consuetudine-De Temporis Supputatione* (Mechliniae: Dessain, 1933), n. 279, 1.

[35] Van Hove, *De Consuetudine-De Temporis Supputatione,* n. 279, 1; *Wernz* (1842-1914)—Vidal (1867-1938), *Ius Canonicum,* Tomus, I, *Normae Generales* (Romae: Apud Aedes Universitatis Gregorianae, 1938), n. 246, note 14.

ARTICLE 3. AS TO MAJOR ORDERS

The intervals between the reception of the several major orders are of three months between subdiaconate and diaconate, and another of three months between diaconate and priesthood. Subdiaconate is the door to the major orders, and represents the choice of a permanent state of life. Once the candidate accepts the obligations of the clerical state, the Code seems to hasten the approach to the priesthood. In proportion as the candidate advances toward the highest grade of the clerical life, the reciprocal offering of God to himself and of himself to God becomes more explicit and irrevocable. With the reception of the subdiaconate, something definite and determinate has been attained.

In accordance with the dignity of sacred orders, and as the realization of even a present participation in the goal still contemplated, sacred orders are to be conferred at the Holy Sacrifice of the Mass.[86] Lending full evidence also to one of the principal parts of the Mass, all those who are promoted to sacred orders are obliged to receive Holy Communion at the ordination Mass.[87]

The value of the interstices is realized more strikingly, perhaps, here than in their application to the lower grades of ordination. If ever the candidate is to be convinced of his vocation and the Bishop to become assured of his worthiness, it is during the periods that are to elapse between the major orders.

There are three possibilities for reckoning the three months' intervals. The Code does not prescribe any definite method to be followed in its statement of the law of interstices. Hence the computations decreed in canons 31-35 and in canon 1006 are to be followed.

The first method of computation according to canon 32, § 2, is the juridical method of reckoning, according to which a month is an interval of thirty days; the second can be made according to the civil calendar, in which the months are taken as they appear in the calendar, as ordained in canon 34; the third calculation is the moral reckoning, that is, the computation of time from one general ordination date to the next. All three are permissible; it

---

[86] Canon 1006, § 2.

[87] Canon 1005.

is only a matter of selecting a computation that is most advantageous for the ordinand or the Bishop.

The first two methods abstract from the correlated dates of the feast days, and hence do not lend themselves to co-ordination with the liturgical calendar. The times of ordination as given in canon 1006 certainly are not precisely timed for the application of the law of interstices. It is, therefore, fitting that the interstices should be adjusted in keeping with the general ordination dates. Whichever general ordination day is nearer the precise reckoning of three months may be reasonably assumed as the logical interval, provided that the general ordination day approximates the interval required by canon 978.

Of the first two computations given, it may be noted here that canon 32, § 2, seems to imply that the juridical month and year (30 and 365 days) are the rule in Canon Law, and that the reckoning according to the civil calendar is exceptional. In practice, however, the computation according to the civil calendar is certainly used more often.[38] In fact, if the juridical method of the reckoning of the months is followed to its conclusion, there is a summation of 360 days which does not represent the juridical year of 365 days.[39]

Blat prefers the computation according to canon 34, § 3, 1°, 3°, namely, that the months are to be taken as they appear in the civil calendar, and not according to the liturgical reckoning. The first day, that of ordination, would not be computed, and the interval would be terminated with the ending of the day of the same date of the third month following the month from which the calculation is initiated.[40]

Cappello favors the liturgical reckoning and states that it fulfills the time required by law. Consequently he holds that an interval from ember day to ember day could be understood as the equivalent of a three months' duration.[41] Cappello appears to

[38] Dubé, *The General Principles for the Reckoning of Time*, p. 130.

[39] Coronata, *Institutiones Iuris Canonici* (5 vols., Taurini: Marietti, 1928-1936), I, 49°, 1. (Hereafter cited *Institutiones.*)

[40] Blat, *Commentarium*, III, pars. I, 329.

[41] "Regula de interstitiis trium mensium inter subdiaconatum et diaconatum atque inter diaconatum et presbyteratum satis observata dicenda, si quis in

present the better view of the method of computing the period of three months, for even if it be granted that the law which requires the intervals is not a liturgical law, surely the law touching the times of ordination is,[42] and it seems that a liturgical computation would fit more smoothly into the observance of the feasts than a reckoning based on a precise number of days. Feasts are variable and not subject to a rigid system of numerical recurrence. Possibly one or two legally specified times as proper ordination dates for the conferring of major orders would have to be foregone if the juridical or civil calendars were used. This is not in keeping with the spirit of ordinations. The Church needs every opportunity for the promotion of ministers. Granted that not every occasion is always used, the fact remains that the way should remain open for the promotion of candidates at the legally appointed seasons. It seems more plausible to say that the Code wished to adjust the ordination dates to the advantage of the ordinand, than that it attempted to co-ordinate the many circumstances regarding ordination for the fulfillment of a certain lapse of time which, even when it has passed, would regularly be outside the times for ordination.

ARTICLE 4. BETWEEN PRIESTHOOD AND EPISCOPACY

The canon on interstices makes no mention of an interval between ordination to the priesthood and episcopal consecration. However, the interval is given in canon 331, which designates the qualifications of a Bishop. The requirement is that the candidate has spent at least five years of service in the priesthood. This term is indeed reasonable if the other qualifications are considered. During this period there is sufficient opportunity for the development on the part of the priest, and observation on the part of his superiors, regarding the qualities required in the Bishop, namely, good morals, piety, zeal for souls, prudence, eminent

---

Quatuor Temporibus subdiaconatus vel diaconatus ordinatus, ordinem superiorem in Quatuor Temporibus sequentibus recipiat, quamvis tres menses non omnino affluxerint"—Cappello, *Tractatus de Sacramentis,* II, Pars III, n. 419.

[42] Canon 1006.

learning, and dispositions that suggest good administrative ability. Also, the allotted interval gives occasion for observance of the practical knowledge of the priest whose activity heretofore in the seminary was confined to the assimilation of principle and theory.

The computation of the interval affords no great difficulty because of its added length. Again the Code has provided a sufficient variety of dates for consecration which should preclude any incompatibility of the *terminus a quo* with the *terminus ad quem* that might result from a physical calendar reckoning. The canon states that the episcopal consecration must be conferred at Mass on a Sunday, or on the feast of an Apostle.[43]

Ayrinhac mentions that this does not include holydays actually or formally of obligation, nor the feasts of Saints Barnabas, Luke or Mark, nor the secondary feasts of the Apostles such as the feast of Saint Peter's Chair or of the Conversion of Saint Paul, but only the anniversary of their death.[44] As justification of his assertion, he refers to a decree of the Sacred Congregation of Rites issued on April 4, 1913. It reads as follows:

D.I. Since the Evangelists are equivalent to the Apostles liturgically, it is asked whether episcopal consecration can be held on the anniversary days of the deaths of Saint Luke and Saint Mark?

D.II. Whether it can be held on the feast of Saint Barnabas?

D.III. Whether a special Papal indult is required for consecration to the episcopate on weekdays a) which are still of precept and consequently are equivalent to Sundays b) or which were once of precept, or suppressed feasts?

R. to I and II: No. R. to III: Yes, to both.[45]

---

[43] Canon 1006, § 1.

[44] Ayrinhac, *Legislation on the Sacraments,* n. 334.

[45] I. Quum Evangelistae in re liturgica Apostolis aequiparentur, quaeritur utrum consecratio episcopalis possit fieri diebus natalitiis Sancti Lucae et Sancti Marci?

II. Utrum fieri possit in festo Sancti Barnabae Apostoli?

III. Utrum speciale indultum Summi Pontificis requiratur ad consecrationem episcopalem peragendam diebus festivis infra hebdomadam (a) qui adhuc sint de praecepto et proinde Dominicis aequiparantur b) vel etiam qui olim erant de praecepto, sive in festis suppressis?

Ad I et II: Negative. Ad III. Affirmative ad utrumque.—*Fontes,* n. 6391.

Cappello explains the *dies natalitius* of canon 1006, § 1, as referring to the liturgical date, i.e., the day of death, and not the natural birthday.[46]

Vermeersch-Creusen maintain that Apostles in this text are to be understood strictly, so that the feasts of Saints Luke, Barnabas, and Mark are excluded.[47]

Cappello sustains in general the affirmations of the other authors, but asserts that consecrations are permitted on the feast of Saint Barnabas because he was an Apostle in the strict sense of the term, having been selected by the Holy Ghost,[48] and also, because the Universal Church gives him the honor and veneration due an Apostle.[49] He upholds this view in the face of the contrary decree of the Sacred Congregation of Rites of April 4, 1913.[50] This opinion hardly seems tenable because the decree forbids consecration on his feast day.

The computation of the five year period is made in accordance with the prescription of canon 34, § 3, 3°. Accordingly, one ordained to the priesthood on Holy Saturday of the year 1943, which occurred on April 24, could be consecrated to the episcopate on or after April 25, 1948 provided the day of the consecration be a Sunday or an Apostle's feast. With an average of more than one possible date per week, there should be no trouble in arranging a consecration date that follows soon after the termination of the five year interval.

ARTICLE 5. REGULATIONS OF THE BISHOP

It is prescribed that during the intervals, the clerics shall according to the Bishop's regulations exercise the orders previously received.[51]

Factually, outside of the seminaries, the orders received in the immediately previous ordination are not by way of universal prac-

[46] "Dicitur *natalitius* liturgice et canonice, non autem naturaliter, cum reapse sit dies obitus, quo nempe e saeculo ad gaudia vitae aeternae convolarunt."—Cappello, *Tractatus de Sacramentis,* II, Pars III, n. 564.

[47] Vermeersch-Creusen, *Epitome,* II, n. 269; Beste, *Introductio in Codicem,* p. 541; Blat, *Commentarium,* III, pars. I, 388.

[48] Acts, xiii, 2.

[49] Cappello, *loc. cit.*

[50] Cf. *supra,* p. 41.

[51] Canon 978, § 1.

tice exercised in the United States. This may be due to the general sufficiency of priests who can assume most of the functions of the lesser orders, and also to the assistance afforded by societies of altar boys, by ushers, janitors and various other lay co-operators who lend their aid to the ministry. In the early Church there was a necessity for special ministers who, as aided by the grace of each successive ordination, performed the duties entrusted to them with prescribed regularity.

However, since the Church has assumed a place of security and recognition in society, most of the duties are now performed by laymen who are available for assisting the priest. The duty of the order of porter is performed by janitors and ushers; the lectorate or the order of reader is assumed by the subdeacon, who generally is moreover, a priest; the functions of the exorcist are discharged by a qualified priest, and then only with special permission of the Ordinary;[52] the duties of the acolyte devolve upon altar boys; the rôles of subdeacon and deacon are fulfilled for the most part by priests.

The question may be raised whether there is an obligation imposed on the ordinand of exercising the order received. Cappello asserts that no strict obligation exists. He maintains that the force of canon 978, § 1, is at most that of a counsel or of a strong urging, but not of a true precept. He affirms that this is the view of authors who commented on the pre-Code law as well as of those who have commented on the Code.[53]

Consequently there is some justification through custom and opinion for the prevalent practice which foregoes the exercise of orders under the regulations of the Bishop. If the Bishops were to insist on this observance, in most cases it would constitute a beneficial exercise for the ordained because of the experience he would acquire, or at any rate such an exercise of orders could constitute an equitable trial for efficiency. Some Ordinaries allow their deacons to assist pastors by preaching the word of God and by distributing Holy Communion. Such exercises are perhaps motivated more as a preparation for the eventual functions in the priesthood rather than as a mode of compliance with the rule of canon 978, § 1.

---

[52] Canon 1151.

[53] Cappello, *Tractatus de Sacramentis,* II, Pars III, n. 421.

CHAPTER IV

Dispensations

ARTICLE 1. JUSTIFICATION OF TERMINOLOGY

The subject of this chapter deals with an extraordinary treatment by the law of the question of interstices, or the law as coming into contact with circumstances that warrant an extraordinary procedure. Previously the law was considered in its native force under ordinary conditions. No effort was made to divert the application of the law from its ordinary course to a situation whereby one might anticipate exceptions. In other words, the law was viewed in its absolute intent and no attempt was made at invoking legal distinctions or at pondering singular instances that might necessitate an altered application of the law. The law was simply contemplated in exclusive accord with its primary import.

The procedure which deviates from the normal case will not be considered as the direct consequence of a dispensation from the law until that status is definitely established, for there are some authors who call into doubt the Bishop's action which is to be considered in this chapter in its nature of a true dispensation. The Code defines a dispensation as a relaxation of the law in a particular case, which relaxation can be granted by the legislator, by his successor in office, by a superior legislator or also by a person delegated by the foregoing.[1]

Reilly states that the term *dispensation* in the science of Canon Law possesses a very limited significance. At present it is used only to signify an act by which for a reasonable cause the obligation of the law is removed in a particular case. At one time this precise meaning did not obtain for the term inasmuch as it signified any exception from the law.[2]

[1] Canon 80.

[2] Reilly, *The General Norms of Dispensation,* The Catholic University of America Canon Law Studies, n. 119 (Washington, D. C.: The Catholic University of America Press, 1939), p. 1 (Cited hereafter as Reilly, *Norms of Dispensation*) ; Brys, *De Dispensatione in Iure Canonico* (Brugis: Beyaert, 1925), p. 16.

Ayrinhac remarks that canonists generally speak of this intervention of the Bishop in the matter of interstices as an act of dispensation, although neither the Council of Trent nor the Code designates it by that term. Then he adds that strictly taken it appears rather like an authorized declaration of the partial or total cessation of the law by reason of a common necessity or utility, whereas the convenience, needs or merits of the ordinand are not mentioned in this connection.[8]

Ayrinhac implies that the general law is not only relaxed, but ceases to exist as a legal instrument in the locality where the conditions for an extraordinary procedure are present. This is hardly tenable, because regardless of how many candidates have been ordained without the observance of the interstices, each succeeding candidate is bound by the law as expressed in the Code. The fact that necessity and utility are present as conditions does not automatically waive the need of observing interstices; even the judgment of the Bishop that these conditions exist does not *ipso facto* remove the ordinand from the orbit of the law. There must be some connection between the Bishop's judgment and his action. The writer maintains that this action is a true dispensation. The establishment of the evidence of necessity and utility are merely the occasions, the reasonable causes that justify the granting of the dispensation. These factors could exist in a diocese for years without one relaxation of the law on interstices. The Bishop must be assured that because these conditions exist, therefore he may lawfully ordain a candidate without observing the interstices. The same course is followed with the next candidate. The Bishop is free to choose whomever he wishes for ordination without the observance of the intervals. The fact remains that the Bishop and the ordinand are subject to the law until necessity or utility permit a lawful relaxation of the law in a particular case. There is a difference between something which ceases to exist at all, and something which ceases to exist with effect and force. In the latter case the law is merely relaxed for certain subjects, but the law remains as a binding force, so that each succeed-

---

[8] Ayrinhac, *Legislation on the Sacraments,* n. 296; Reilly, *Norms of Dispensation,* p. 71.

ing subject is bound until a dispensation has been granted. For all other subjects, the obligation continues.

The mere fact that the Code does not use the term *dispense* in the canon on interstices does not warrant the conclusion that a dispensing power has not been employed. There can be no doubt of a clear delegation of power in canon 978, paragraph 2. This is obvious from the very definition of such a power. An *explicit* concession of faculties to dispense is sustained whenever a superior clearly indicates such a power either by the definite terms of a law or a special indult, or by means of some other sign which distinctly expresses it.[4]

Paragraph 3 of canon 978 states that special permission of the Roman Pontiff is necessary for the conferring of minor orders together with the subdiaconate, or of two sacred orders on the same day. Accordingly the Bishop has no power from the Code to act according to his own discretion under any and every given set of conditions. On the contrary, the Bishop is given power to act, under certain conditions, against the law in regard to the interstices between the various minor orders and between the various sacred orders. That he may lawfully contravene a law under certain circumstances is sufficient to establish the existence of his dispensatory power.

ARTICLE 2. THE ASCERTAINING OF NECESSITY AND UTILITY

Canon 978, § 2, asserts that the intervals between the order of acolyte and the order of subdeacon, and between the various sacred orders are to be observed unless the necessity or the utility of the Church in the Bishop's judgment demands otherwise. Gasparri alleged that in his day the Church was suffering a universal need for priests, and therefore, in practically every case, the condition of utility or of necessity was verified. In any event, he asserted that the aspirant always had to presume that the dispensation granted by the Bishop was licit.[5]

---

[4] Coronata, *Institutiones,* I, 107; Michiels, *Normae Generales Iuris Canonici* (2 vols., Lublin, Polonia: Universitas Catholica, 1929), II, 480.

[5] Gasparri indicated specific reasons for dispensing. According to his view, necessity was present if there was a shortage of priests to carry on the work of the ministry in a particular church of the diocese, or if others

Reiffenstuel considered utility as a factor which was verified whenever the candidates for ordination possessed extraordinary qualifications. He took the view that it was not enough to have a sufficiency of workers or even a surplus, if they were not outstanding. Consequently, he allowed the shortening of the intervals for a candidate if he showed promise of adding prestige to the clerical state in the community, or if he gave indication of raising the standards whereby the work of the Church was to be enriched and rendered more fruitful. Under the heading of necessity he included not only the reason of a deficiency of priests, but also a situation wherein the duties incumbent on the priests could not otherwise be adequately fulfilled, or the liturgy of the Church carried out in its entirety and fullness of beauty through lack of available officers. These conditions could exist not only when capable priests were wanting, or when a greater number was necessary for the satisfaction of the ordinary needs of the Church, but also even when there was a sufficient number of priests ordained, but they did not reside in the localities where they were needed, either because of other legitimate occupation or because of indisposition or disability. He did not base his opinion on the number of priests in a diocese taken indiscriminately without reference to their condition, but rather on the possible aggregate of available ministers. As a reason for this view he stated that necessity and utility were not of an indivisible character, that is to say, the interpretation of these terms had to yield to an appraisal affected also by extrinsic considerations and qualifications, so that the extension of their application in any given situation was to be determined within the measure of a discreet moral judgment and a discriminate prudent estimate.[6]

Pirhing regarded necessity and utility as personal rather than as local causes. He did not put so much emphasis on the needs of

---

already ordained could not be spared to supply the existing need by assuming the duties connected with it together with their own proper commissions and obligations; utility was a reason if there was a lack of scholarly priests, or if there was a candidate who was of advanced age and notable for his learning.—Gasparri, *De Sacra Ordin.*, I. n. 504; Many, *De Sacra Ordin.*, n. 108.

[6] ". . . non consistit in indivisibili, sed moraliter dijudicari debet secundum arbitrium boni viri."—Reiffenstuel, lib. I, tit. 11, n. 151.

the diocese as in the Bishop's judgment that the candidate was vitally necessary or useful regardless of the condition of the diocese.[7]

Cappello maintains that necessity and utility as mentioned in canon 978 are to be understood in a spiritual sense, and consequently should be interpreted broadly. This view admits any cause that could be interpreted as favoring the good of souls, such as the filling of a sacred office, the administration of the Sacraments and sacramentals, the celebration of Mass, and the discharge of other functions of the same nature. Therefore, any factor involving a spiritual effect constitutes a motivating cause for a dispensation of the interstices.[8]

The acceptance of this opinion would really serve to enervate the legal force and authoritative import of the canon. The possibilities are so great under the view adopted by Cappello that a dispensation would practically always be in order, and the Bishop would be given a quite arbitrary power to use his dispensing faculty. This view is hardly in keeping with the spirit of the law of interstices. The Code in determining the general causes for dispensation wished to impress upon the Bishop that the ordinary course of preparation and study should be permitted to mature, unless in special cases the Church would reap a greater benefit from a relaxation of the law. The fact that the burden of arriving at a decision as to the course of action rests on the Bishop's conscience is considered in the law as sufficient for insuring a correct motivation; the moral admissibility of the act of dispensation is to be determined by the Bishop himself. But it must be remembered that something positive must be ascertained as a reason by the Bishop in his act of judgment. The permanently available reasoning that he is head of a diocese wherein he has the care of the spiritual welfare of souls, and, that therefore any spiritual object regardless of its significance and importance warrants an extraordinary procedure on his part, can not be sustained as in accord with the intent of the law.

---

[7] Pirhing, lib. I, tit. 11, n. 91; Barbosa, pars. II, alleg. XVIII, n. 5.

[8] ". . . necessitas vel utilitas in casu est *spiritualis* eaque *moraliter* et *lato sensu* accipienda."—Cappello, *Tractatus de Sacramentis,* II, Pars III, n. 335.

Schmalzgrueber offered an extended list of causes which could constitute a sufficient motive in his time.[9]

The opinions of Gasparri, Reiffenstuel and Pirhing are preferable. They are definite in their application, and they are not as extreme as Cappello's since they are founded on cognizable fact rather than on rationalized suppositions. Any other causes for waiving the observance of the interstices will be adequate only insofar as they can be reduced to necessity or utility under the views adopted above.

It is not clear what is to be understood by the word *Church* in relation to which the necessity or utility must be determined.[10] Certainly the Universal Church can not be meant, since then the existence of a local cause would in effect be in force as a universal cause in every case of promotion to higher orders. Nor could the intent of the law be directed towards any individual church taken as a separate unit without relation to the diocese as a whole.[11] Gasparri believed that under the name *Church*, there was indicated the Diocese for which the candidate was to be promoted, and in which he was to exercise the sacred ministry.[12]

Canon 969 gives a clue when it rules that no secular should be ordained unless he be necessary or useful in the judgment of the

---

[9] "1. Si ordinandi sint referendarii utriusque signaturae, familiares papae, vel canonici cathedralium, aut collegiatarum ecclesiarum, vel earum adjutores. 2. Si iidem sint magistri, h. e. doctores, licentiati, vel etiam baccalaurei ss. theologiae, vel doctores, aut licentiati utriusque aut saltem canonici juris, et in publica et approbata universitate ejusmodi aliquam consecuti; ut etiam si triennio ss. theologiae studiis sedulam navarunt operam. 3. Si beneficium habeant, quod sacerdotalem ordinem exigit, vel aliud perpetuum, aut etiam cappellaniam ad tempus vitae sibi concessam, ut illi deservire per seipsos possint. 4. Ob penuriam sacerdotum saecularium, vel regularium, in provincia, dioecesi, vel monasterio. 5. Ob solatium patris, vel matris. Debent tamen isti, ut ex hac causa dispensare episcopus in interstitiis possit, excessisse annum aetatis 50. 6. Si ipse ordinandus 26 annum excesserit: quo tamen casu, ut etiam in praecedente, si dispensationem quoad interstitia petens per triennium saltem in habitu clericali honeste et laudabiliter vixerit."—Schmalzgrueber, lib. I, tit. 11, n. 14.

[10] Canon 978, § 2—". . . nisi necessitas aut utilitas Ecclesiae, iudicio Episcopi, aliud exposcat."

[11] Ayrinhac, *Legislation on the Sacraments*, n. 282.

[12] Gasparri, *De Sacra Ordin.*, I, n. 504; Many, *De Sacra Ordin.*, n. 108.

Bishop *for the churches of the diocese.* The Bishop, after all, must have the general welfare of the souls submitted to his care in mind for all his actions.[13] Therefore he will adopt a general outlook when reviewing any necessity or utility. This does not mean that he cannot regard the elements existing in a particular church of the diocese as a sufficient motive for the granting of the dispensation. Certainly the diocese is constituted of territorial units or parishes. But he should analyze a particular situation with a view to the constituted whole. Thus every situation is to be viewed as diocesan in scope, and individual cases are to be considered only insofar as a diocesan need is created. Accordingly no one particular church should be given a special consideration to the detriment of the other churches.

Beste asserts that any plausible cause suffices.[14] This generality appears to be juridically vulnerable. Such an unqualified statement entails the same difficulties as those which were mentioned in the treatment of Cappello's view as given above. If the Code were precise enough to comprise the dispensatory causes under two definite categories, it hardly seems justifiable to treat of still another category which was left unmentioned by the law.

ARTICLE 3. PRELATES WHO CAN DISPENSE

A. Prior to the Code

a. Bishop of Incardination

As was observed above, the law of interstices as it appears in the decrees of the Council of Trent was not so stringent as not to contemplate a relaxation of the law. In regard to the ordination of seculars, the faculty to dispense was granted to the respective Bishops only for instances when they were ordaining their proper subjects, so that a Bishop could not dispense from the interstices when ordaining non-diocesans with dimissorials.[15]

---

[13] Canons 335, § 1; 336, § 2; 343, § 1.

[14] Beste, *Introductio in Codicem,* p. 527.

[15] Fagnanus, II, *de temporibus ordinationum et qualitate ordinandorum,* cap. *Litteras,* n. 1; Reiffenstuel, lib. I, tit. 11, n. 153; Pichler, lib. I, tit. 11,

Reiffenstuel argued that the reason for this assertion was to be found in the text of the decrees of the Council. He maintained that the Council of Trent granted the faculty only to the Bishop of the diocese in which the candidate was incardinated, since he alone knew principally whether the causes of utility or of necessity existed in his diocese, and accordingly was best qualified to make a reasonable judgment regarding them; the power to dispense the intervals was not conceded to the ordaining Prelate if he was not the candidate's superior, since he resided outside the diocese, was unacquainted with its particular need, and hence was not capable of making a competent judgment.[16] Through observation, examination and association, the Bishop of incardination maintained vigilance and disciplinary discretion over all candidates subject to him in his territory, while the ordaining Prelate was at most executing a favor for the Diocese of the candidate in fulfilling the petition to ordain. The only connection the latter had with the ordinand was effected through the knowledge gained from the letters which authorized the ordination and through the personal contact occasioned by the ceremony of the ordination. He certainly was in no position to make a judgment or to ascertain the existence of a reasonable cause for a dispensation from the interstices through such slight information.

Added support is lent to this opinion in another session of the Council of Trent. There it was explicitly decreed that "no one ought to be ordained who in the judgment of his Bishop is not useful and necessary to his Church."[17] The words "of his Bishop" corroborate the view that the ordaining Prelate as such could not waive the requirement of the interstices, for the decree specified that the Bishop whose diocese the candidate was to serve was also the one to determine whether the candidate was useful or necessary.

---

n. 12; Suarez (1548-1617), *Opera Omnia* (28 vols., ed. L. Vivès, Parisiis, 1856-1861), XVI, 168, n. 21; Wernz, *Ius Decretalium,* II, n. 70; Many, *De Sacra Ordin.,* n. 112; Gasparri, *De Sacra Ordin.,* I, n. 506; S.C.Ep. et Reg., *Aliphana,* 9 aug. 1593—*Fontes,* n. 1487.

[16] Reiffenstuel, *loc. cit.;* ". . . unless the Bishop should deem it more expedient to act otherwise"; ". . . unless necessity or the utility of the Church shall in the judgment of the Bishop require otherwise."—Conc. Trident., sess. XXIII, *de ref.,* c. 11, 13, 14; Schroeder, pp. 171, 172, 173.

[17] Conc. Trident., sess. XXIII, *de ref.,* c. 16; Schroeder, p. 173.

This opinion prevailed throughout the period from the Council of Trent to the codification of the law in the Code. There is evidence that doubt continued as to the power of the ordaining Prelate, but there is no decree contrary to the prevailing opinion which was adopted as the correct interpretation of the decrees of the Council of Trent. Not until 1909 was an extension of this faculty made to the ordaining Prelate. The question was submitted to the Congregation of the Sacraments, which after due deliberation gave a favorable opinion which was referred to the Roman Pontiff for approval. The Holy Father confirmed the decision of the Congregation of the Sacraments that Ordinaries authorized by indult to ordain *extra tempora,* or without observing the interstices might use these faculties in favor of strangers who were presented to them for ordination with dimissorial letters from their Ordinary.[18]

It is evident from this response that the matter was never altogether definite and certain, but it is also clear that the decree was decidedly an innovation, for it was referred to the Holy Father as an extraordinary decree for his approval. It reveals that the practice was that which had been followed after the Council of Trent through the adoption of the views of the authors cited above. Moreover, it implies that a special faculty was granted, and therefore that it did not rule out the opinion that by the law of the Council of Trent it was the Bishop of incardination who had the faculty to dispense, and that only by way of special permission was the ordaining Prelate competent to dispense. Thus the situation remained unchanged in substance even after the decree of 1909, namely, that the Bishop of incardination could dispense by virtue of the power granted in the decrees of the Council of Trent on the interstices, while the ordaining Prelate could not apart from a special faculty given outside the law.

Moreover, the granting of a dispensation implied an act of jurisdiction.[19] This power of jurisdiction could be exercised directly only over subjects. The ordaining Prelate, when he was not

---

[18] S.C. de Sacramentis, *Friburgen.,* 15 aug. 1909—*AAS,* I (1909), 656: *Fontes,* n. 2098.

[19] Gasparri, *De Sacra Ordin.,* I, n. 506; Many, *De Sacra Ordin.,* n. 167; Reilly, *Norms of Dispensation,* p. 2.

the Bishop of incardination, had no jurisdiction over the ordinand in the matter of ordination since there was no superior-subject relationship between the ordaining Prelate and the candidate. Accordingly a superior-subject relationship had to exist before any claim to a dispensatory power over an individual person could be substantiated.[20] The ordaining Prelate when dispensing by reason of the decree of the Sacred Congregation of the Sacraments issued August 15, 1909, was dispensing merely by virtue of authority and power which have been specially communicated to him. The right to ordain in view of the reception of dimissorial letters did not of itself include the right to dispense from the interstices.[21]

The Bishop could dispense either expressly or tacitly. In knowingly promoting a candidate to a higher order before the lapse of the interval allotted by law and without mention of a dispensation, the Bishop was understood to dispense tacitly or *ipso facto*.[22] However, the Bishop was not presumed to have dispensed tacitly if he promoted a candidate to a higher order without observing the lapse of the full interval, but also, without having knowledge that he was acting in an extraordinary case.[23] This interpretation was important because of the penalties that might otherwise have been incurred. Pirhing asserted that without at least a tacit dispensation the ordinand was liable to the penalties levied for the non-observance of the interstices.[24]

b. The Ordaining Bishop

There was some indecision whether the decrees of the Council of Trent regarding the intervals of ordination included regulars. Their status was settled by various decrees of the Sacred Congregation of the Council, which decided that regulars were subject to

[20] Reilly, *Norms of Dispensation*, p. 95.

[21] Gasparri, *De Sacra Ordin.*, nn. 80, 219, 245.

[22] Barbosa stated that every canonical impediment from which the Bishop could dispense was presumed to be taken away when the Bishop knowingly acted contrary to the normal and usual requirement if there was no express dispensation.—Barbosa, pars. II, alleg. XVIII, n. 7; Pirhing, lib. I, tit. 11, n. 91; Reiffenstuel, lib. I, tit. 11, n. 156.

[23] Barbosa, *loc. cit.;* Reiffenstuel, *loc. cit.*

[24] Pihring, *loc. cit.*

the ordaining Bishop for dispensation from the interstices. The ordaining Bishop was identified as the Bishop of the diocese in which the religious house was situated.[25]

The decrees and decisions did not apply, however, to those regulars who had a special apostolic privilege, either by direct concession or by an act of participated inter-communication, of receiving orders *extra tempora* on three consecutive Sundays or feast days, or even within a prescribed shorter period, and who were consequently excused from the observance of the interstices; for in regard to these the Holy Father himself issued the dispensation, and thus they did not need any further dispensation, not even from their own superior, though he perhaps enjoyed the faculty to dispense.[26]

Reiffenstuel maintained that the right of the ordaining Bishop followed from the decrees of the Council of Trent, wherein the faculty of dispensing from the interstices was expressly committed to the judgment of the Bishop, and the Regular Prelates were not included under the title of Bishop.[27]

---

[25] ". . . cum petitum esset si Regulares praefato decreto comprehenderentur, respondit 'comprehendi' ".—S.C.C., *Mediolanen.*, 1573, as cited by Many, *De Sacra Ordin.*, n. 167; S.C.C., *Aquen.*, mense iul. 1589, ad. 1, 2: "Dubitatur, quia dispensatio est actus iurisdictionis, utrum Episcopus possit dispensare super dictis interstitiis et temporum spatiis cum Regularibus coram se constitutis ad ordines suscipiendos cum dimissoriis suorum Superiorum. Et si respondeatur, posse, non obstante quod dicti Regulares sint de alia Dioecesi et exempti: quaeritur utrum pro causa dispensandi sufficiat dictorum Superiorum fides attestantium ita expedire. Ad 1. Congregatio Concilii respondit, posse, si ita ei visum fuerit expedire. Ad. 2. Sufficere. *Fontes*, n. 2209; S.C.C., *Brugnaten.*, 17 maii 1593: "Congregatio Concilii censuit iudicium hoc, remittendi temporum interstitias, ad Episcopum solum pertinere, non autem ad Generales, aut Provinciales Ordinum; et Regulares concurrentibus debitis requisitis, teneri recipere ordines ab Episcopis, in quorum dioecesibus sunt Monasteria, in quibus ipsi degunt." —*Fontes*, n. 2257; S.C.C., *Nullius*, 31 maii 1597: "Congregatio Concilii censuit remissionem interstitiorum etiam quoad Regulares ex causis tantum a Concilio expressis faciendam pertinere ad Episcopum ordinantem; eum tamen hac in re debere quoad causas deferre iudicio et attestationi Superioris Regularis ordinandi."—*Fontes*, n. 2311; S.C.C., *Savonen.*, 1 iul. 1597 —*Fontes*, n. 2316; S.C.C., 12 sept. 1609—*Fontes*, n. 2379.

[26] Reiffenstuel, lib. I, tit. 11, n. 40.

[27] ". . . verba sunt intelligenda secundum proprium significationem, simulque, in potiori significatione accipienda, ubi de opposito non constat."—

The question may be raised whether the Bishop could refuse to grant the dispensation if he was asked by the Religious Superiors. Barbosa maintained that, if there was a just cause for dispensing, the Bishop was bound under pain of mortal sin to dispense the petitioner, especially if scandal would otherwise have followed; or if suspicion of an impediment would have been aroused.[28] On the other hand, Suarez contended that if a Superior granted dimissorials for the promotion of a candidate to orders, and made no mention of a dispensation from the intervals, the Bishop could not, solely on his own judgment and by his own will, dispense from the interstices.[29]

In the light of the views expressed above by Barbosa, Pirhing and Suarez, the writer's opinion is that the Bishop was not free

---

Reiffenstuel, lib. I, tit. 11, n. 158; Barbosa said that nowhere in the decrees of the Council of Trent could be found any reference to such a faculty given to Regular Superiors. Bishops, however, had to accept the Superior's judgment since it belonged to the religious Superior to judge about and to provide for the utility or the necessity of his order; in general, those who sent candidates elsewhere for ordination made the judgment as required by the Council of Trent—Barbosa, pars. II, alleg. XVIII, n. 10; Pirhing asserted that exempt religious could subject themselves to the Bishop for the dispensations or absolutions to be received.—Pirhing, lib. I, tit. 11, n. 90; Many stated that the Bishop who dispensed Regulars was not necessarily the Bishop of the diocese in which they lived, but the *ordaining* Bishop since they could be sent outside the diocese for ordination under certain conditions.—Many, *De Sacra Ordin.*, n. 167; Wernz, *Ius Decretalium,* II, n. 70.

[28] Barbosa, pars. II, alleg. XXXII, n. 51. According to Pirhing the Bishop had to grant the dispensation if the Superior asked for it—Pirhing, *loc. cit.;* Suarez stated that the Bishop could refuse, but not licitly without a reasonable cause—Suarez, *Opera Omnia,* XVI, 169, n. 23.

[29] ". . . quia omnis facultas simpliciter data, debet in reliquis omnibus intelligi secundum jus." Suarez concluded that this dispensation *in rigore* pertained rather to the religious superior who issued the dimissorials and asked for the dispensation rather than to the ordaining Bishop: ". . . nam, licet uterque concurrere deberet, tamen, acceptatio ex parte ordinantis magis videtur pertinere ad usum dispensationis quam ad valorem ejus; . . . ergo quantum est ex se, seu quantum ad actum primum (ut sic dicam) per quem persona fiat habilis et sine impedimento, potestas episcopalis quoad hanc dispensationem videtur extendi ad Prelatos religiosos, quamvis ipsi modestiae causae recte faciant non tam utendo verbo dispensandi, quam rogandi Episcopis in litteris dimissorialibus quas conferent, ut admittant suos subditos ad ordines, non servatis interstitiis, quia sufficiens necessitas vel utilitas intercedit"—Suarez, *Opera Omnia,* XVI, 169, n. 23.

to act arbitrarily in the matter, but there had to be a concurrence of petition and concession, so that the two principals were understood to be in agreement. There was no justifiable reason for a groundless and unwarranted exercise of power. If the Bishop wished to grant a dispensation, he was to petition the Superior for accord and consent. If no basis for a dispensation was forthcoming from the Religious Superior, the Bishop was bound to proceed according to the ordinary force of the dimissorial letters.

c. The Vicar Capitular

The faculty of dispensing from the interstices, as granted to the Bishop by the Council of Trent, was extended by various decrees of the Sacred Congregation of the Council to the Vicar Capitular during the vacancy of the see.[30] Gasparri asserted that the Vicar Capitular could dispense from the interstices only in those cases in which he could give permission to his diocesan subjects to receive orders, or, in other words, in which he could grant dimissorial letters.[31] Pallottini, in citing a response of the Sacred Congregation of the Council alleged that the Vicar Capitular did not have the faculty of waiving the observance of the intervals until a year after the vacancy of the see.[32] Gasparri thus accorded with the response cited by Pallottini, namely, that the Vicar Capitular could not grant dimissorials until a year after the see had become vacant.[33] Consequently, the Vicar Capitular could not

---

[30] Barbosa, pars. II, alleg. XVIII, n. 6; Gonzalez-Tellez, lib. I, tit. 11, cap. 15, n. 8; Many, *De Sacra Ordin.*, n. 112; S.C.C., *Asturicen.*, 21 apr. 1591, ad 1—*Fontes*, n. 228; S.C.C., *Brugnaten.*, 17 maii 1593—*Fontes*, n. 2257.

[31] Pichler, lib. I, tit. 11, n. 12; Pirhing, lib. I, tit. 11, n. 89; Schmalzgrueber, lib. I, tit. 11, n. 13; Gasparri, *De Sacra Ordin.*, I, n. 506.

[32] Pallottini, s.v. "Sacramentum Ordinis," V, n. 49 (S.C.C., in *Acherutana*, maii 1602).

[33] "It shall not be lawful for chapters of churches, when a see is vacant, to grant, either by a provision of the common law or by virtue of a privilege or custom, permission to be ordained or dimissorial letters . . . within a year from the day of the vacancy . . ." Conc. Trident., sess. VII, *de ref.*, c. 10; Schroeder, p. 59.

dispense from the interstices except when he could grant the dimissorials.

In regard to the dispensation of regulars during the vacancy of the see, the Regular Superior had the right to send his subjects to any Bishop for ordination, and this Bishop could therefore grant the dispensation.[34]

d. Religious Superiors

Suarez maintained that if a Religious Superior was permitted to ordain by reason of a special Apostolic privilege, he also could dispense from the interstices for the orders he was authorized to confer. This did not follow from the jurisdiction he enjoyed as a Religious Superior, but from the special concession which was extended to him insofar as he had the power of ordaining.[35]

e. Abbots *de regimine*

Abbots *de regimine,* if they were authorized to confer tonsure and minor orders on their regular subjects, were likewise empowered to dispense from the observance of the interstices, as long as they observed the conditions specified by the Council of Trent. The reason was that Abbots who thus ordained exercised an episcopal authority over their subjects; moreover, having been granted the principal power, namely that of conferring orders, which power was proper to Bishops, the authority to dispense from the observance of the interstices was also understood to have been granted them by accession.[36]

The power of Abbots to confer tonsure and minor orders was

---

[34] Many, *De Sacra Ordin.,* n. 167.

[35] Suarez, *Opera Omnia,* XVI, 168, n. 21. Pirhing held as a probable opinion with Schmalzgrueber that if the exempt Religious Superior who had quasi-episcopal jurisdiction over his subjects could grant dimissorials for major orders, he could also dispense from the observance of the interstices for these orders.—Pirhing, lib. I, tit. 11, n. 90; Schmalzgrueber, lib. I. tit. 11, n. 13; Gonzalez-Tellez, lib. I, tit. 11, cap. 15, n. 8.

[36] Barbosa, pars. II, alleg. XVIII, n. 3; Reiffenstuel, lib. I, tit. 11, n. 159.

evidenced in the Decretals of Gregory IX,[37] and in the decrees of the Council of Trent.[38]

f. Prelates *Nullius*

Many declared that the Bishop of the nearest diocese was the superior authorized to dispense from the observance of the interstices for the subjects of a Prelate *Nullius,* since all matters pertaining to the ordination of these subjects were committed to him by the Council of Trent.[39] As to the verification of the cause of the dispensation, however, the Bishop had to adhere to the attestation of the Prelate.[40]

B. After the Code

a. Bishop of Incardination

The Bishop is extended more power of dispensation by the law of the Code than was previously granted by the Council of Trent. The Code permits the Bishop to dispense the interval before priesthood either because of necessity or because of usefulness, while the Council's legislation was more restrictive, demanding the simultaneous existence of both reasons.[41]

---

[37] C. 11, X, *de aetate et qualitate et ordine praeficiendorum,* I, 14.

[38] "It shall not be lawful in the future for abbots . . . however exempt, residing within the limits of a diocese, even in case they are said to be of no diocese or exempt, to confer the tonsure or minor orders on anyone who is not subject to them."—Conc. Trident., sess. XXIII, *de ref.,* c. 10; Schroeder, p. 170.

[39] Conc. Trident., sess. XXIII, *de ref.,* c. 10; "Quoad seculares subditos praelatis . . . *Nullius,* dispensatio in interstitiis pertinet, non ad praelatos, sed ad episcopum viciniorem. Ratio est quia totum negotium ordinationis horum subditorum commissum est a Concilio Tridentino huic episcopo."—Many, *De Sacra Ordin.,* nn. 61, 112; Gasparri, *De Sacra Ordin.,* I, n. 508.

[40] Pallottini, s. v. "Sacramentum Ordinis," V, nn. 43, 44 (in *Nullius Putignani,* iunii, 1592).

[41] Canon 978, § 2: After stating the interval, the Code demands that it be permitted to run its full course ". . . nisi necessitas *aut* utilitas Ecclesiae, iudicio Episcopi, aluid exposcat." The decree of the Council of Trent reads ". . .. nisi ob ecclesiae utilitatem *ac* necessitatem aliud episcopo videtur . . ." Conc. Trident., sess. XXIII, *de ref.,* c. 14; Schroeder, p. 444.

The interstices for tonsure, for the minor orders and for the subdiaconate remained unchanged by the legislation of the Code. However, the intervals of a year between subdiaconate and diaconate, and between diaconate and priesthood were reduced to periods of three months each in the Code.[42]

The Code, in designating the recipient of the dispensatory power, uses the same words without definition as did the Council of Trent. The simple statement, "in the judgment of the Bishop," points to the active subject of the dispensatory power in both legislations. The writer's conclusions on this point are in agreement with the doctrine which existed before the Code, namely, that the Bishop of incardination is alluded to here. Ayrinhac avers that the Bishop who enjoys this power of dispensation in particular cases is the Bishop of the candidate's domicile.[43]

At first impression this opinion seems safe enough, since it appears tantamount to a declaration that the proper Bishop for ordination in accordance with canon 956 is the Bishop who dispenses the interstices. But the same canon makes mention of candidates who are incardinated in another diocese by first tonsure. The obvious conclusion, in accordance with Ayrinhac's view, is that the proper Bishop for ordination as mentioned in canon 956 can also dispense from the observance of the interstices for a candidate who has ceased to be subject to him because of his incardination in another diocese. However, in the matter of promotion to ordination, the candidate in the latter case is no longer subject to the Bishop of his domicile. All preliminaries such as the granting of dimissorial letters, of dispensations, etc., are now within the power of the Bishop of the diocese for which the aspirant has been promoted. This is supported by a private reply of the Pontifical Commission of Interpretation as issued on December 7, 1931. The Bishop of Santa Fe in Argentina asked this Commission whether one who has been promoted to first tonsure by his proper Bishop, but for the service of another diocese, and who has by that very fact become incardinated in the latter diocese in accordance with c. 111, § 2, and the reply of the same Commission

---

[42] Canon 978, § 2; Conc. Trident., sess. XXIII, *de ref.*, c. 13, 14; Schroeder, p. 172.

[43] Ayrinhac, *Legislation on the Sacraments*, n. 296.

of 17 August, 1919, *ad* II, should receive the higher orders from the former Bishop, or rather from the Bishop of the diocese in which he is now duly incardinated, even though he be obliged to finish his theological studies in another diocese. The reply stated that the candidate should receive the higher orders from the Bishop of the diocese in which he is duly incardinated.[44] The natural and obvious meaning of this reply is that, as soon as incardination has taken place through first tonsure, the proper Bishop for the conferring of the higher orders on the cleric is the Bishop of incardination, who is not necessarily the Bishop of the cleric's domicile.

Further defense is offered by two promulgated decisions of the Pontifical Commission for the Interpretation of the Code issued July 24, 1939. They read as follows:

D.I. Whether a layman who is promoted to first tonsure by his proper Bishop for the service of another determinate diocese with the consent of its Bishop, is incardinated in this latter diocese according to the rule of canon 111, § 2.

R. Yes.

D.II. Whether the Bishop of the diocese for the service of which a layman has been promoted to first tonsure by his own Bishop, has the proper and exclusive right to confer orders on him, or to give dimissorial letters for his ordination according to the rule of canon 955, § 1, even though he has not yet acquired a domicile in the same diocese.

R. Yes.[45]

The *dubium* specifically states that the tonsured cleric has not yet acquired a domicile in the diocese of destination, and yet the

---

[44] *PCI,* Private resp., 7 dec. 1931, as reported in Bouscaren, *The Canon Law Digest,* II, 51.

[45] D.I. An laicus, qui a proprio Episcopo ad primam tonsuram promotus sit in servitiam alius determinatae dioecesis de consensu huius Episcopi, huic dioecesi incardinatus sit ad normam canonis 111, § 2. R. Affirmative.

D.II. An Episcopus dioecesis, in cuius servitium laicus ad primam tonsuram a proprio Episcopo promotus fuerit, ille iure proprio et exclusivo ordines conferre aut litteras dimissorias dare valeat ad norman canonis 955, § 1, licet ipse in eadem dioecesi domicilium nondum acquisiverit. R. Affirmative.—*PCI,* 24 iul. 1939 (AAS, XXXI (1939), 321). Cf. Bouscaren, *The Canon Law Digest,* II, 52 and 238.

reply attributes to the Bishop of incardination the proper and exclusive right to confer orders himself, or to authorize any other Bishop through dimissorial letters to confer orders on his incardinated cleric. This puts an end to the possible confusion of two proper Bishops for the one cleric.

Though the *dubium* asked only about those who were immediately incardinated into alien dioceses through first tonsure, it is quite certain that the same solution must avail those clerics who are formally incardinated into an alien diocese before promotion to the priesthood.

The obvious result of this decision is that canon 956 must be understood to refer to the initial tonsure of laymen only, and canon 111, § 2 must be considered as settling the identity of the proper Bishop for clerics even as regards their ordination to higher orders.[46]

Vermeersch-Creusen and Cappello state the bare fact that the proper Bishop is the Bishop who is authorized to dispense from the observance of the interstices.[47] This is true if they mean the proper Bishop by incardination, and not the proper Bishop for ordination as mentioned in canon 956.

The proper Bishop for ordination as mentioned in canon 956 merely decides which Bishop is entitled to confer tonsure on laymen. As soon as tonsure is conferred, attachment to a definite diocese automatically follows, and when a cleric is attached to a Bishop's diocese, no other Bishop may assume the authority to ordain him. This makes the Bishop of incardination not only a proper Bishop, but the exclusively proper Bishop for ordination.[48]

Beste states that either the proper Bishop, or the Bishop who ordains a non-diocesan with dimissorials, can dispense with equal power, and refers to the decree of the Sacred Congregation of the Sacraments issued August 15, 1909, in defense of his assertion.[49]

---

[46] McBride, *Incardination and Excardination of Seculars,* The Catholic University of America Canon Law Studies, n. 145 (Washington, D. C.: The Catholic University of America Press, 1941), p. 370.

[47] Vermeersch-Creusen, *Epitome,* II, 244; Cappello, *Tractatus de Sacramentis,* II, Pars III, n. 335.

[48] McBride, *Incardination and Excardination of Seculars,* p. 360.

[49] Beste, *Introductio in Codicem,* p. 527; S.C. de Sacramentis, 15 aug. 1909—*AAS,* I (1909), 656.

The first and obvious criticism is that he is not specific enough in identifying the proper Bishop with the Bishop of incardination. Then, too, he fails to mention that according to the wording of the decree the ordaining Bishop can dispense non-diocesans with dimissorials only because he has been granted a special faculty to that effect. It must be remembered that the law of the Council of Trent and also canon 978 of the Code refer only to the Bishop of incardination in regard to seculars. Any other Bishop who can dispense does so through the accession of a special privilege and outside the general law.

b. The Ordaining Bishop

The Bishop who is to grant the dispensations for religious, even those who are exempt, is the Bishop who has the right to receive the letters of ordination. Reference is restricted here to religious who do not enjoy the privilege of being ordained without the observance of the interstices.[50]

The Ordaining Bishop must submit to the attestation of the religious superior of the ordinand regarding the verification of the causes for the dispensation.[51] There is no problem if a Bishop other than the principal mentioned in the dimissorial letters ordains, since in these letters not only the Ordinary of the Diocese is granted the faculty to ordain, but also any other Bishop in communion with the Holy See. If the religious is directed to another Bishop for ordination, that Bishop would have the right to dispense the interstices if so petitioned.[52]

---

[50] Canon 965: "Episcopus ad quem superior religious litteras dimissorias mittere debet, est Episcopus dioecesis, in qua sita est domus religiosa, ad cuius familiam pertinet ordinandus"; Canon 966.

[51] Cappello, *Tractatus de Sacramentis,* II, Pars III, n. 420; Vermeersch-Creusen, *Epitome,* II, n. 429; Ayrinhac, *Legislation on the Sacraments,* n. 296; Beste, *Introductio in Codicem,* p. 527.

[52] ". . . Nos tenore praesentium facultatem ei conferimus, ut ab Excmo et Revmo Ordinario Nostro vel, eo annuente, ab alio quocumque Episcopo, communionem cum Sede Apostolica habente, . . . ordinari valeat."—Beste, *Introductio in Codicem,* p. 514.

c. The Vicar Capitular

The Vicar Capitular is restricted by law from exercising any faculty concerning ordination within the first year of the vacancy of the see, except in behalf of those who must be promoted to orders in view of a benefice already conferred upon them, or soon to be conferred, or also, in view of their being needed to fill a diocesan office, appointment to which brooks no delay.[53] Therefore the Vicar Capitular can not dispense from the observance of the interstices within the first year of vacancy, except for the special circumstances and under the conditions mentioned in canon 958, § 1, 3°.

d. Religious Superiors

Religious Superiors petition the ordaining Bishop for a dispensation from the observance of the interstices.[54]

e. Abbots *de regimine*

Abbots *de regimine* are limited as to the power to ordain, both in regard to the passive subject of ordination and also in regard to the orders to be conferred. Outside these limits the orders are invalid, unless the Abbot has the episcopal character. The restrictions as to the passive subject of ordination are that at least by simple profession he be a member of the monastery of which the Abbot is the Superior. The Abbot, moreover, must be a priest and must have received the abbatial blessing.[55] Under these provisions he can confer the first tonsure and the minor orders, and accordingly can dispense from the observance of the interstices for these orders.

f. Other Prelates

Vicars and Prefects Apostolic, Abbots and Prelates *nullius*, if they have the episcopal character, are equal to diocesan Bishops

[53] McBride, *Incardination and Excardination of Seculars*, p. 303.

[54] Cf. *supra*, pp. 53-56.

[55] Canon 964, 1°.

in the matter of ordination.[56] Consequently they may dispense from the observance of the interstices under the conditions already delineated in the sections which treat of the power of the Bishop of incardination,[57] and of the ordaining Bishop.[58] If they do not enjoy the episcopal character, they can confer only tonsure and minor orders validly, both on their own subjects and on strangers who are presented to them with dimissorial letters.[59]

ARTICLE 4. APOSTOLIC INDULT

Definite limitations of the Bishop's power to dispense from the observance of the interstices are specified in canon 978, § 3. There it is decreed that without a special permission of the Roman Pontiff minor orders and subdiaconate, or two major orders, cannot be conferred on a candidate on one and the same day. Furthermore, it is not even lawful to confer the tonsure and one of the minor orders, or all minor orders on a candidate in one day.[60]

Recourse to the Holy See must be made in each instance for the lifting of the former limitations, and under ordinary conditions for each dispensation from the latter. For seculars the competent Roman Congregation is the Sacred Congregation of the Sacraments; for religious the Sacred Congregation for Religious; and the Sacred Congregation for the Propagation of the Faith is to be petitioned by all who are under its jurisdiction.[61]

---

[56] Canon 957, § 1.

[57] Cf. *supra,* pp. 50-53; 58-62.

[58] Cf. *supra,* pp. 53-56; 62.

[59] Canon 957, § 2.

[60] Canon 978, § 3: Nunquam tamen, nisi de peculiari licentia Romani Pontificis, minores ordines cum subdiaconatu duove sacri ordines uno eodemque die . . . conferantur; imo nec primam tonsuram conferre licet una cum aliquo ex ordinibus minoribus, neque omnes ordines minores una simul.

[61] Canon 249; It was asked which of the Congregations was competent in regard to dispensations for the receiving of sacred orders by religious. The Special Commission of Cardinals provided for by canon 245 replied: "The Sacred Congregation for Religious."—Competency of S.C. de Rel. (Special Commission of Cardinals), 24 martii 1919, as reported in Bouscaren, *The Canon Law Digest,* I, 161. Cf. *AAS,* XI (1919), 251; canon 252, § 3.

Blat maintains that the concession of the faculty to confer two sacred orders on one day, or minor orders together with the subdiaconate, is an extraordinary one which lies beyond the ordinary faculties of the Sacred Congregations. The grant would have to be made directly by the Roman Pontiff, because of the words of the canon, "never without a special permission of the Roman Pontiff," or through the Sacred Congregations with the specific approval of the Roman Pontiff.[62]

It is evident that the prohibition in the former restriction is more exacting than in regard to the conferring of tonsure with one of the minor orders, or of all the minor orders simultaneously.[63]

There is no occasion for the canonical fiction mentioned above with reference to the conferring of two sacred orders on the same day,[64] because of the reckoning of the day which is fixed at 24 hours to be computed from midnight to midnight.[65] Also, the possibility of joining an ordination in the evening with an ordination on the following morning to constitute a day by a canonical fiction is precluded because Mass may not be celebrated in the evening,[66] and ordination to sacred orders may not be conferred outside of Mass.[67]

---

[62] Canon 244; Blat, *Commentarium,* III, pars. I, 329.

[63] Cappello, *Tractatus de Sacramentis,* II, Pars III, n. 419; Vermeersch-Creusen, *Epitome,* II, 249.

[64] Cf. *supra,* pp. 18-20.

[65] Canon 32, § 1; Blat, *loc. cit.*

[66] Canon 621, § 1: Missae celebrandae initium ne fiat citius quam una hora ante auroram vel serius quam una hora post meridiem.

[67] Canon 1006, § 2: "ordinationes in sacris celebrentur intra Missarum sollemnia. . . ."

CHAPTER V

The Interstices and the Requisites for Licit Ordination

A review of the development of the interstices bears out the admonition given at the beginning of this study, namely, that a direct treatment of the institute, to be practical, needs to be supplemented by a study of its incidental relations to other parts of the Code. A review of the lone canon in the Code which regulates the interstices reveals, indeed, a set of rules to serve as a guide in determining the intervals, but the determination must ultimately be made in the light of a more definite and exacting legislation. At first hand, one might be led to suppose a deficiency in the Code, if he were to neglect seeking a further understanding of the subject from the general legislation on sacred orders.

A complete presentation of the law on the interstices is offered only if one maintains contact with other parts of the treatise on orders which, taken as a whole, complements the canon on the interstices and affords an orderly and clear legal pattern of the institute. Only then will it be manifest that the canon on the interstices, far from being a disabling factor in the law, constitutes rather a central point in the law the aim of which is to place other conditions for ordination in their proper order and sequence. A complete assembly of the various legal enactments is essential for a clear and precise application of the law, and for the establishment of a practicable viewpoint founded on reason. Consequently, it has become desirable to change the focus of the present treatise from the interstices as such to the connecting links between the interstices on the one hand, and the requisite canonical age, the required course of studies and the prescribed retreats before ordination on the other. The discussion of these elements will proceed in the order given. If the legal provisions affecting these preparatory requisites are observed in conjunction with the observance of the law of the interstices, there will follow the establishment of clearly serviceable norms for determining the intervals in the light of the intention of the legislator.

Obviously, there should be no effort made at this point to give a complete treatment of any of these prerequisites for ordination. They will be touched upon only in their effect on the interstices.

ARTICLE 1. THE INTERSTICES AND THE CANONICAL AGE

Canon 975. *Subdiaconatus ne conferatur ante annum vicesimum primum completum; diaconatus ante vicesimum secundum completum; presbyteratus ante vicesimum quartum completum.*

The canon determining the years for the canonical age makes no mention of the period which is required to elapse before the reception of tonsure and the minor orders, but the studies which these ordinations presuppose indicate the maturity and experience necessary, and so implicitly point also to the purpose underlying the interstices, which are thus implicitly sanctioned.[1] Even the canon treating the course of studies does not fix a specific age for the reception of tonsure and the minor orders, but it does determine the reaching of a state of maturity which adequately fulfills the purpose of the interstices. The legislator is content that the candidate will receive tonsure and the minor orders only after the inception of his theological course, and is assured that even though a mature age has not been reached, at least the preparation for higher theological learning has given the assurance of the attainment of definite and necessary intellectual qualifications.

Thus one can observe that the equipment required by the Code for the lower orders is not so much a matter of emphasis on a specific age, as of a period reached in the intellectual preparation for the priesthood. There is no admission here of any inability to determine the age precisely for the lower orders, but rather there is reflected in the demand an assurance that the subject is ready at a definite point in his training. Exact determinations of age are postponed until the choice of sacred orders is offered the aspirant. Accordingly, there can be no conflict or disagreement between the canonical age and the intervals in regard to the re-

[1] Canon 976, § 1, forbids the reception of tonsure until after the inception of the theological course.

ception of the lower orders, for the interstices can be determined without reference to any qualification of a specific age in the candidate for orders.

With the reception of major orders, however, there is occasion for a comparison between separate pieces of legislation. The interval prescribed as requisite between the subdiaconate and the diaconate is one of three months according to canon 978, § 2, whereas it could be as much as one full year according to canon 975 if the candidate did not have the required age for the reception of the deaconship. The direct legislation on the interstices allots three months for the interval between diaconate and priesthood, while the canon fixing the canonical age decrees a passage of two years for those who are ordained deacons at the completion of their twenty-second year. It must be remembered that the canon decreeing the canonical age for major orders deals with minimum age requirements, and there is nothing absolute about the demand which the law makes. However, in canon 978, § 2 there is an absolute requirement which applies uniformly to all candidates for orders, whether they have reached the earliest possible age required or not.

However, the two provisions fit together perfectly. If the time element based on the usual educational courses is traced, the ordinand will be found to have attained the age of twenty-four years when he is ready to be called to the subdiaconate, and twenty-five years at the time he is to receive the order of priesthood. This calculation is based on the inception of primary training at the age of six. Thus the student will have finished his elementary training at an estimated age of thirteen years. Add to this the four-year course dedicated to the secondary or high school period, and the two-year duration of the preparatory seminary training, and the candidate at their completion will have attained the age of nineteen years. The further requirement of two years of philosophy will place the candidate in his majority of twenty-one years at the completion of the course of philosophy. Subdiaconate is not to be conferred until the end of the third year of theology, diaconate not before the inception of the fourth, and priesthood not until the first semester of the fourth year is completed.[2] So, on the basis of this computation the subdeacon at the time of his ordina-

[2] Canon 976, § 2.

tion will usually be twenty-four years of age, and the deacon twenty-five years old. The latter would also be approximately the age of the candidate for ordination to the priesthood.

The above stated reckoning considers the date of birth as falling within the summer season before each fall school term. Thus the date of birth is arbitrarily placed as near as possible to the school year in order to make the computation as general in application as possible. There is, of course, a possibility of an earlier beginning of school life than at the age of six years, but whatever probability there may be to the contrary will in general rather favor a more advanced age than that used for a starting point in the above calculation.

The ages required for promotion to sacred orders are based by the legislator on the period of life when the candidate is in a position to make a decision in a fully responsible manner. Since for a licit ordination there is required that development of body and mind which renders the candidate capable of a voluntary and free acceptance of his ordination and of a due understanding of the duties annexed to each order, a certain age is prescribed by ecclesiastical law which, in its consideration of all contingencies, presumes that development of body and mind to be present.[3] This object compares well with the purpose of the interstices, so that it is in order here to emphasize again that the legislation for the canonical age is formulated to co-ordinate with the law of the interstices, rather than to subordinate it merely to its own demands.

No need for a dispensation will have to be anticipated if the ordinary educational course is followed. Moreover, authors state that the Holy See is not wont to dispense from the requirement of age for the subdiaconate, and rarely dispenses from the required age for the diaconate.[4]

[3] Wernz-Vidal, *Ius Canonicum,* Tomus II, *De Personis* (Romae: Apud Aedes Universitatis Gregorianae, 1934), n. 219.

[4] Ayrinhac *(Legislation on the Sacraments,* n. 290) states that the Church is ready to grant dispensations from twelve to eighteen months for the priesthood, but rarely from more. Cappello *(Tractatus de Sacramentis,* II, Pars III, n. 407) asserts that if indults are given to dispense from a year, they are to be understood of the priesthood. Cf. Vermeersch-Creusen, *Epitome,* II, n. 245.

There is not possible any discrepancy of interpretation in regard to the calendar to be used in the computation of the interval for the canonical age, such as was encountered in the determination of the interstices themselves. However, no conflict need be anticipated in adjusting the two calendars which regulate the requirements for the interstices and the canonical age.[6] It is necessary that the reckoning of the age be precise and definite in all cases to avoid any confusion and also, that there be the added satisfaction of the assurance of a common and invariable marker. Authors agree that the calendar for the computation of the canonical age is the civil calendar, and the reckoning is to be made according to canon 34, § 3, 3°. Canon 975 demands the completion of the year which it indicates as requisite for each sacred order. Thus the date of birth is not computed inasmuch as the moment of birth ordinarily does not coincide with the beginning of the day.. Accordingly, the year will expire with the end of the last day bearing the same numerical date. For illustration, one born on May 16, 1920, could not be ordained to the priesthood until May 17, 1944.

Thus, as has been observed, no conflict between the intervals demanded in canon 975 and those required in canon 978 will ordinarily arise with the possible exception in relation to the age required for the priesthood, which requirement readily yields to dispensation as long as the discrepancy from the required age is not of a disproportionate duration.

ARTICLE 2. THE INTERSTICES AND THE REQUIRED COURSE OF STUDIES

Canon 976, § 1. *Nemo sive saecularis sive religiosus ad primam tonsuram promoveatur ante inceptum cursum theologicum.*

§ 2. *Firmo praescripto can. 975, subdiaconatus ne conferatur, nisi exeunte tertio cursus theologici anno; diaconatus, nisi incepto quarto anno; presbyteratus, nisi post medietatem eiusdem quarti anni.*

Some discussion of the relation of the course of studies to the interstices has already been presented, inasmuch as it is practically

[6] Cf. *supra*, pp. 33-38.

a co-incident matter for the discussion regarding the canonical intervals to involve also a consideration of the required course of studies.[6]

The entire theological course contemplates a period extending to forty-five months. This takes into consideration a nine month period for each scholastic year together with a three months' vacation at the end of each of the first three years.[7] Ayrinhac asserts that to be a theological student in the sense of canon 1365 one must have completed the philosophical course as prescribed by law, and have commenced the course of theology which includes Dogmatic, Moral and Pastoral Theology, Scripture, Church History, Liturgy, Canon Law, Homiletics and Ecclesiastical Chant. According to his view it would not suffice, for example, to attend some lectures on Homiletics or Chant, or to study privately some theological treatise during the years devoted to the study of philosophy. But he considers the requirements of the law fulfilled if the student has completed the philosophical course, and follows besides, some theological courses in a clerical seminary. Thus the candidate would be qualified for the reception of tonsure after having completed his course of philosophy under these conditions.[8]

The above expressed opinion seems an unwarranted interpretation of the words *ante inceptum cursum theologicum.* More in harmony with the rule of canon 976, § 1 is the opinion of Cappello, namely, that the theological course is begun only with the actual matriculation in the normal theological course, but before the actual beginning of classes in theology.[9]

The inception of the theological course seems to indicate the enrollment in a clerical seminary with the avowed purpose of studying theology, rather than a combination of both philosophy

---

[6] Cf. *supra,* p. 28.

[7] A scholastic year is to be taken as consisting of nine months according to a definition of the Sacred Consistorial Congregation—S.C. Consist., 24 martii 1911, ad I—*AAS,* III (1911), 181; Ayrinhac, *Legislation on the Sacraments,* n. 292; Beste, *Introductio in Codicem,* p. 526; cf. *The Jurist* (Washington, D. C.: The School of Canon Law, The Catholic University of America, 1941-   ), I (1941), 153, 154.

[8] Ayrinhac, *loc. cit.*

[9] Cappello, *Tractatus de Sacramentis,* II, Pars III, n. 414.

and theology during the period devoted principally to philosophy. Even at the conclusion of this combined study the student would still be faced with the duty of four years of theological study as required in the Code.

Since there are no prescribed interstices for the reception of tonsure and the minor orders according to canon 978, the usefulness of canon 976, § 1, as a point of initial reckoning is evident. By dating the conferring of tonsure on the basis of the inception of the theological course, the time for the conferring of the minor orders is rather easily determined by a flexible schedule.

A review of the author's opinions in regard to the requirement of the conferring of subdiaconate towards the end of the third year of theology demonstrates that they favor such an extension as would allow this ordination to fit smoothly into the plan of the liturgical calendar. Cappello interprets the phrase *exeunte tertio cursus theologici anno* as permitting ordination to the subdiaconate within thirty or forty days before the completion of the school year.[10] Ayrinhac permits ordinations at Pentecost, for example, even though the school year closed several weeks later.[11] Blat favors the view which lends its approval for ordinations at Easter in addition to Pentecost, regardless of the number of days involved.[12]

Authors are agreed that the school year must cover a period of nine months inclusive of the tests and examinations at the end of the scholastic year.[13] However, they permit a wider interpretation in the matter of ordination, and regard the actual termination of the lecture courses even though the general examinations have not been held as marking within the realm of what is allowable, the end of the year or the close of the semester.[14]

Deaconship cannot be conferred until after the beginning of the fourth year in the theological course. Cappello gives a twofold interpretation without rejecting either. He places the begin-

---

[10] *Tractatus de Sacramentis,* II, Pars III, n. 414.

[11] *Legislation on the Sacraments,* n. 292.

[12] *Commentarium,* III, pars. I, 327.

[13] Vermeersch-Creusen, *Epitome,* II, 246; Cappello, *loc. cit.;* Ayrinhac, *loc. cit.*

[14] Vermeersch-Creusen, *loc. cit.;* Cappello, *loc. cit.;* Blat, *loc. cit.*

ning of the year either at the time of the enrollment, even though it be a month or more before the actual call to lecture courses, or at the undertaking of class work.[15]

Vermeersch understands the scholastic year as the total space of time during which lectures are given.[16]

Priesthood may not be conferred until after the first semester of the fourth year of theology. This rule places the date of ordination to the priesthood five months, or at least four and a half months, after the actual beginning of class work.[17]

Vermeersch sets the time for this ordination at the beginning of the second semester, and Augustine agrees with this.[18]

There may seem to be a lack of conformity between the two three-month intervals established between the subdiaconate and the diaconate, and between the diaconate and the priesthood in canon 978, and the periods decreed for these ordinations according to the required course of studies. If the subdiaconate were conferred at the actual ending of the school year and ordination to the diaconate were held a month before the opening of the fourth year, the mere fact of an approximation of the three-month interval could undoubtedly be observed. However, the minimum of three months must be increased between deaconship and priesthood in that case to meet the requirement that the ordination to the priesthood take place only after the first term of the fourth year. These previous statements are made for the purpose of a comparison of the two legislations based on an effort to arrange their objects in absolute accord without resorting to extraordinary faculty.

It has been the practice for certain religious communities to ordain their subjects to the priesthood after three years of theology through a proper dispensation which requires these subjects to complete the course of studies after their ordination to the priesthood. According to a declaration of Pope Pius XI, issued Oc-

---

[15] Cappello, *loc. cit.*

[16] Vermeersch-Creusen, *loc. cit.*

[17] Cappello, *loc. cit.*

[18] Vermeersch-Creusen, *loc. cit.;* Augustine, *A Commentary on the New Code of Canon Law* (8 vols., St. Louis: B. Herder, vol. IV, 3. ed., 1925), nn. 458, 459.

tober 23, 1923, all dispensations for ordinations anticipated in this fashion are granted under the condition that the newly ordained priests shall complete the fourth year of theology, and that they shall not be employed in the care of souls, in preaching, in the hearing of confessions, or in any other work outside the religious community which would interfere with their studies. Superiors have a grave obligation in conscience to see that these conditions are complied with, and they apply to all dispensations, no matter in what form they were issued or granted after the promulgation of the Code.[19]

Cappello applies this norm to the anticipated ordination to the priesthood of seculars with a similar dispensation. However, he interprets the declaration as forbidding only the frequent or habitual exercise of the ministry, but not the occasional exercise, *per modum actus,* e.g. by assistance during week-ends in parishes. Apparently he understands a frequent or habitual exercise as implying daily assistance in view of his interpretation of the occasional exercise. Moreover, he restricts the prohibition of the exercise of the ministry, as contained in the declaration, to the scholastic year and not to the period of vacation.[20]

ARTICLE 3. THE INTERSTICES AND RETREATS BEFORE ORDINATION

Canon 1001, § 1. *Qui ad primam tonsuram et ordines minores promovendi sunt, spiritualibus exercitiis per tres saltem integros dies; qui vero ad ordines sacros, saltem per sex integros dies vacent; sed si qui, intra semestre, ad plures ordines maiores promovendi sint, Ordinarius potest exercitiorum tempus pro ordinatione ad diaconatum reducere, non tamen infra tres integros dies.*

§ 2. *Si, expletis exercitiis, sacra ordinatio qualibet de causa ultra semestre differatur, exercitia iterentur; secus iudicet Ordinarius utrum iteranda sint, necne.*

To accomplish the purpose of the interstices, it is not sufficient that one await the attainment of the necessary physical, intellectual and moral qualities through the passage of time, and of a com-

---

[19] S.C. de Religiosis, declar. 27 oct. 1923—*AAS,* XV (1923), 549.

[20] Cappello, *Tractatus de Sacramentis,* II, Pars III, n. 415.

mendable submission to discipline, but there must be evidence of a spiritual development and of a right intention with a proportionate regard for the sacredness of the calling. This effect reaches its climax in spiritual retreats, the definite and immediate spiritual preparation for each sacred ordination.

The period set aside for this purpose before ordination to tonsure and the minor orders consists of three full days. A full day, according to canon 32, § 1, consists of twenty-four consecutive hours to be computed from midnight to midnight. Cappello, however, does not favor a rigid computation, but rather prefers a moral computation which would allow the omission of an hour or two without changing the juridical quantity of a whole day.[21]

Six full days of retreat are required before each ordination to a sacred order, but if the candidate is to receive several major orders within six months, the Ordinary may reduce the days of retreat before deaconship, but not to less than three full days.[22] Cappello permits the reduction even if the period extends a few days beyond six months.[23] He also maintains that there is no question of a dispensation if, according to canon 1001, § 2, the Ordinary rules that the retreat is not to be repeated. There is question, then, merely of a declaration to that effect, since there is no question of relaxing the law inasmuch as the law does not prescribe a repetition unless the Ordinary requires it.[24]

New understanding of canon 1001 was given by a reply to a question submitted by the Archbishop of Vrhbosna (Sarajevo) on April 27, 1928, to the Sacred Congregation of the Sacraments, and by means of the accompanying official comments which were also published. The question was proposed whether, in the mind of the legislator, the requirement of canon 1001, § 1, was to be observed strictly, even in a case where all the sacred orders are conferred on a candidate within a very short time, for example,

---

[21] Cappello, *Tractatus de Sacramentis,* II, Pars III, n. 552.

[22] The Ordinary mentioned in canon 1001, § 1, 2, for exempt clerical religious will be either the ordaining Ordinary or the religious Ordinary. As a rule it will be the latter.—Keene, *Religious Ordinaries and Canon 198,* The Catholic University of America Canon Law Studies, n. 135 (Washington, D. C.: The Catholic University of America Press, 1942), p. 66.

[23] Cappello, *loc. cit.*

[24] Cappello, *Tractatus de Sacramentis,* II, Pars III, n. 553.

within a month. The reply stated that canon 1001, § 1, was to be observed, namely, that it mattered little if the candidate received all the major orders within six months or one month, the Ordinary could reduce the time of the retreat before deaconship, but not below three full days. However, if by Apostolic permission or by a decree of the Bishop, for a grave cause in accordance with canon 1006, § 3,[25] with the observance of all the requirements of law, especially those of canons 975-978, sacred orders are conferred on distinct, consecutive or proximate days, so that there is no time to observe the prescriptions of canon 1001, § 1, in that case, provided that the sacred order which is first conferred always be preceded by spiritual exercises for at least six full days, the other orders, if in the judgment of the Bishop according to canon 1001, § 2, it can be done, shall be preceded by at least one day of spiritual retreat. Pope Pius XI ratified and approved the above reply in an audience given May 1, 1928.[26] Moreover, as stated in the published official comments, the reply was given in conformity to the intent of canon 1001, § 1, and was simply declaratory of the existing law.[27]

Ordinarily this situation could arise under a Bishop's decree only after the first semester of the fourth year, since the necessary requirements of age and of the course of studies must be met, and no dispensatory faculty is granted as to either in the laws themselves. The interstices may be dispensed with under the conditions specified in canon 978, § 2. Thus, for instance, if the sacred ordinations were compressed within three days, all that is prescribed is six full days of retreat before ordination to subdeaconship, and the continuance of the retreat until after ordination to the priesthood. A day's retreat both before diaconate and priesthood is decreed, but even this may be omitted if the Ordinary so judges.

Cappello declares that the same reply can be used in the cases where only two ordinations are held, e.g., to the subdiaconate and

[25] Canon 1006, § 3: "Gravi tamen causa interveniente, Episcopus potest eas habere etiam quolibet die dominico aut festo de praecepto."

[26] S.C. de Sacramentis, *Romana et Aliarum,* 27 apr. 1928—*AAS,* XX (1928), 359-362.

[27] Cf. *Animadversiones* to the above reply, n. 5.

the diaconate, or to the diaconate and the priesthood with a brief interval interposed. He applies it also to minor orders. So, for example, if they are conferred a few days after tonsure, the three days before tonsure will suffice for the retreat for the minor orders together with one day of retreat preceding each ordination date. If this preceding day cannot be inserted without difficulty, the Ordinary may omit it also. Cappello also applies the rule of the three days' retreat before minor orders to the retreat preceding subdeaconship if it followed within a few days, so that just three full days would have to be added in order to suffice for the retreat for major orders.[28]

Even though it was stated[29] that the preceding reply was merely a declaration of existing legislation, it must be admitted that it is a distinct innovation in practice which has a definite bearing on the prescribed interstices. It allows a shortening of the intervals as much as the law permits without danger of conflict with the legislation on retreats, so that even the greatest necessity may be obviated without recourse to Rome.

---

[28] Cappello, *Tractatus de Sacramentis,* II, Pars III, n. 552.

[29] Cf. *supra,* p. 76.

CHAPTER VI

Exceptions and Sanctions

ARTICLE 1. CUSTOM

After the Council of Trent the custom of conferring all the minor orders at the same time was admitted,[1] and also the custom of promoting to tonsure together with all the minor orders on the same day obtained.[2]

Even the custom of conferring minor orders and subdiaconate on the same day was recognized as licit where it was in practice.[3] However, it was not the practice of the Roman Curia to grant faculties to confer all minor orders and subdiaconate on the same day. In other words, the custom where it was in practice was tolerated, but the practice was not encouraged by any dispensation.[4]

In the Code of Canon Law there is express reprobation of any custom which would permit the conferring of minor orders together with subdiaconate, or of the reception of two sacred orders

---

[1] Fagnanus (II, *de temporibus ordinationum et qualitate ordinandorum*, cap. *De eo*, nn. 23, 26, 35) stated that the custom of conferring minor orders without observing the interstices was a custom *praeter ius*, not *contra ius*. Cf. Pirhing, lib. I, tit. 11, n. 83; Reiffenstuel, lib. I, tit. 11, n. 160; Schmalzgrueber, lib. I, tit. 11, n. 15; Gasparri, *De Sacra Ordin.*, I, n. 510.

[2] Barbosa, pars. II, alleg. XI, n. 19; Pirhing, *loc. cit.;* Gasparri, *ibid.;* Wernz, *Ius Decretalium*, II, n. 70; Many, *De Sacra Ordin.*, n. 108.

[3] Barbosa, pars. II, alleg. XIV, n. 5; Gonzalez-Tellez, lib. I, tit. 11, cap. 15, n. 11; according to Fagnanus *(op. cit.*, n. 41) this was a custom *contra ius*. Cf. Reiffenstuel, lib. I, tit. 11, n. 167; Schmalzgrueber, *loc. cit.;* Gasparri, *loc. cit.;* Wernz, *loc. cit.;* Many, *De Sacra Ordin.*, n. 114.

[4] Where the custom of conferring minor orders and subdiaconate on the same day was not in practice, the Sacred Congregation of the Council reprehended such a procedure.—S.C.C., *Boven.*, 29 ian., 12 febr., 10 apr., 7 maii 1707—*Fontes*, n. 3046; S.C.C., *Calaritana*, 21 febr. 1728—*Fontes*, n. 3337.

on the same day.[5] With the advent of the Code these customs had to be corrected as corruptions of the law, even though they were of the longest duration, nor can they be revived in the future, since their very entrance upon a potential period of possible temporal prescription remains perpetually excluded.[6]

The conferring of tonsure along with one of the minor orders or together with all the minor orders simultaneously is forbidden, but the possible formation of a contrary custom seems admitted under the terms of canon 5.[7] Cappello feels that such a contrary custom is not legitimate in practice, since there does not seem to be any solid reason for tolerating such a custom.[8] Cappello's view seems the more reasonable inasmuch as there is no occasion for conferring tonsure and minor orders together except in one or the other cases wherein there is no time to defer the reception of these lesser orders in order to observe the prescribed intervals. However, authors admit that under these conditions, even when the centenary custom has been suppressed, *epikeia* may be used whereby the legislator is presumed to suspend the law when an extraordinary case arises in which the strict observance of the law would result in something unexpectedly harmful or very exceptionally burdensome.[9]

ARTICLE 2. PRIVILEGES

In regard to privilege, Pope Gregory XIII (1572-1585) granted to the General of the Jesuits abundant faculties to dispense from

---

[5] Canon 978, § 3: "Nunquam tamen, nisi de peculiari licentia Romani Pontificis, minores ordines cum subdiaconatu duove sacri ordines uno eodemque die, reprobata quavis contraria consuetudine, conferantur . . ."

[6] Canons 5; 27, § 2. Cf. Guilfoyle, *Custom,* The Catholic University of America Canon Law Studies, n. 105 (Washington, D. C.: The Catholic University of America, 1937), pp. 74, 106.

[7] Canons 5 and 978, § 3—Insofar as they are centenary customs not rejected and condemned by the Code, they may be tolerated if the Ordinaries judge that they cannot prudently be abolished because of the local circumstances and the peculiarities of the people. Cf. Vermeersch-Creusen, *Epitome,* II, n. 249.

[8] Cappello, *Tractatus de Sacramentis,* II, Pars III, n. 419.

[9] Vermeersch-Creusen, *loc. cit.;* Cappello, *loc. cit.*; Reilly, *Norms of Dispensation,* p. 2.

the interstices. This privilege was granted with a clause which forbade other religious orders to share in it by way of intercommunication between them and the Jesuit Order.[10]

A controversy arose whether regulars shared in this privilege regardless of the prohibiting clause. Reiffenstuel, representing the more probable opinion, stated that other regulars did share in this privilege.[11] Many seems to have supported the opposite opinion.[12]

However, a preceding Pontiff could not limit the power of his successors, as is evident from the conduct of the subsequent Popes. Gregory XIV (1590-1591) granted a direct participation in all of the Jesuits' privileges to the Cistercians and to the Crozier Fathers.[13]

Clement VIII (1592-1605) in 1596 granted to the Congregation of Saint John the Evangelist in Portugal the same privileges conceded by Gregory XIII to the Jesuits.[14]

Again, Clement VIII in 1597 communicated to the Franciscans of the Minor Observance all privileges howsoever granted or to be granted to all other orders, whether Mendicants or not.[15]

---

[10] Gregorious XIII, const. *"Pium et utile,"* 22 sept. 1582: ". . . ipsos etiam absque ulla functione in ordinibus ipsis, interstitiorumque ad illos suscipiendos observatione . . . proprii ordinarii licentia et aliis requisitis, ad minores, ac etiam extra tempora a iure statuta, tribusque dominicis vel aliis festis diebus, etiam continuis, ad sacros etiam presbyteratus ordines promoveant, ac sic illi omnibus requisitis praediti essent. Nos enim illis ordines omnes praedictos sic suscipiendi, ac praedictis antistibus eos ipsis conferendi facultates tribuimus"; "Praesentis autem gratiae communicationem omnibus aliis, etiam qui sua privilegia cum ipsa Societate copiose participant, participareque poterunt, quomodolibet in futurum fieri prohibemus"—*Bull. Rom. Taur.*, VIII, 398.

[11] Reiffenstuel, lib. I, tit. 11, n. 51.

[12] "Quoad communicabilitatem, attendendum est ad clausulas."—*De Sacra Ordin.*, nn. 166, 168.

[13] Gregorius XIV, const. *"Illius qui,"* 21 sept. 1591—*Bull. Rom. Taur.*, IX, 479.

[14] "Item Patribus Congregationis S. Joannis Evangelistae Portugaliae concessit Clem. VIII de mense Novemb. 1596 ut possint ordinari extra tempora et per quemcumque Episcopum tribus Dominicis, vel festivis diebus continuis, vel interpollatis non servatis interstitiis."—Clement VIII as cited in Barbosa, pars. II, alleg. XVII, n. 7.

[15] Clemens VIII, const. *"Pastoralis Officii,"* 20 dec. 1597—*Bull. Rom. Taur.*, X, 388.

Benedict XIII (1724-1730) in the Council of Rome which was convened in 1725 argued that all regulars had these privileges, and asserted that he wished all these exemptions, whether granted expressly or through participation with others, to remain in force.[16]

Moreover, Benedict XIII in 1727 granted directly to the Order of Preachers privileges similar to those granted to the Jesuits by Gregory XIII.[17] Therefore, even if the other regulars did not participate by intercommunication in the privileges granted by Gregory XIII to the Jesuits, they did participate by intercommunication in the privileges granted to the religious cited above according as they participated generally in the privileges of the latter.

After the reestablishment of the Society of Jesus, its Superiors were again granted the privilege of presenting their candidates for ordination without the observing of the interstices.[18]

In regard to religious with simple vows, the Redemptorists were given the perpetual privilege to promote their candidates without observing the interstices.[19]

All the privileges cited above are still in effect, since there is no revocation of them in the Code of Canon Law.[20]

---

[16] "Quo vero ad Regulares privilegia a summis Pontificibus habentes, sive expresse sive per viam communicationis concessa, sacros videlicet Ordines extra tempora suscipiendi, cum privilegia ipsa in suo robore persistant, nec iis derogatum fuisse constet, decernimus proinde, Regulares eosdem absque novo indulto Apostolico tuto posse extra tempora ordinari."—*Coll. Lac.*, I, 354, b.

[17] Benedictus XIII, const. "*Pretiosus*," 25 maii 1727—*Bull. Rom. Taur.*, XXII, 322.

[18] Leo XII, const. "*Plura inter*," 11 iulii 1826—*Bull. Rom. Taur.*, XVI, 449.

[19] Pius VI, const. "*Sacrosanctum apostolatus officium*," 21 aug. 1789—*Bullarii Romani Continuatio Summorum Pontificum* (19 vols., Prati, 1756-1883), VI, 2111 (Hereafter cited, *Bull. Rom. Cont.*); Pius VII, const. "*Qui sicut boni*," 9 ian. 1807—*Bull. Rom. Cont.*, VII, 887.

[20] Canon 4: ". . . privilegia . . . quae ab Apostolica Sede ad haec usque tempora personis sive physicis sive moralibus concessa, in usu adhuc sunt nec revocata, integra manent, nisi huius Codicis canonibus expresse revocentur." Cf. Schaefer, *De Religiosis ad Normam Codicis Iuris Canonici* (3. ed., Romae: Typis Polyglottis Vaticanis, 1940), n. 457.

ARTICLE 3. PENALTIES

There was no penalty decreed in the law of the Council of Trent for the failure of the Ordinary to observe the interstices, or for the ordained, either as a censure or as an irregularity.[21] Sixtus V (1585-1590) was the first to take up the question of penalties after the Council of Trent. He was most strict in regard to the interstices, and in 1589 decreed numerous penalties against the ordaining prelate who violated the Church's law in this matter.[22]

Recognizing in the Constitution of Sixtus V a danger to the Church in the reduction of the number of ordinations through fear of the multiplication of penalties by the ordaining prelates, Clement VIII in 1596 restored the legislation of Pius II (1458-1464) in regard to the sanctions attached to the law of the inter-

---

[21] Barbosa, pars. II, alleg. XVIII, n. 11; Pirhing, lib. I, tit. 11, n. 91; Reiffenstuel, lib. I, tit. 11, n. 203.

[22] Sixtus V, const. *"Sanctum et Salutare,"* 5 ian. 1589, § 2: "Ut igitur Praesules Ecclesiarum intelligant, si in re tam gravi, et tanti momenti, culpa aut negligentia peccaverint . . . praesenti Constitutione perpetuo statuimus, et ordinamus, ut si in posterum Antistes aliquis . . . aut non servatis temporum interstitiis, ita ut aliquis unico die, seu continuatis diebus ad plures ordines Sacros, vel post unum ordinem susceptum, sine causa rationabili antequam tempus ab eodem Concilio Tridentino praefixum elabatur ad alium ordinem promoveatur, sine dispensatione, aut indulto Apostolico, Clericali caractere non legitime insigniverit, aut ad ordines minores, vel Sacros, ut praefertur, vel alias male promoverit, sive id scienter, sive ignoranter fecerit, nisi debita diligentia adhibita iustus error, et probabilis facti ignorantia eum excuset, ut in quo deliquit in eo puniatur, a collatione quorumcumque ordinum, atque adeo ipsius tonsurae, et ab executione omnium munerum Pontificalium, eo ipso suspensus, et ab ingressu Ecclesiae interdictus existat, aliisque gravioribus poenis nostro, et pro tempore existentis Rom. Pontificis arbitrio puniatur. Quod si spreta huiusmodi suspensione, et interdicto, in praemissis se temere ingesserit, etiam a regimine, et administratione suae Ecclesiae, seu Monasterii, et a perceptione fructuum mensae eiusdem, ac quorumcumque beneficiorum per eum, in titulum, vel commendam, seu alias obtentorum suspensionem eo ipso incurrat; eiusque interdicti, aut suspensionis relaxationem, aut poenarum remissionem ab alio, quam a Rom. Pontifice pro tempore existente nequeat obtinere."—*Fontes,* n. 166.

stices, which after the Council of Trent were no longer in force, and rescinded the Constitution of Sixtus V.[23]

Penalties for the violation of the observance of the interstices were revoked by the Constitution *"Apostolicae Sedis"* of Pius IX on October 12, 1869.[24]

The Code of Canon Law makes no mention of a penalty for the non-observance of the interstices. Of course, this does not mean that Ordinaries can contravene the interstitial law with impunity. There is always the vigilance and surveillance of the Metropolitan who is bound to manifest all abuses to the Holy See for judgment. This precaution should secure habitual observance of the law.[25]

---

[23] Clemens VIII, const. *"Romanum Pontificem,"* 28 febr. 1596—*Fontes,* n. 182; Pius II, const. *"Cum ex sacrorum,"* 17 nov. 1461: ". . . auctoritate Apostolica . . . statuimus, et ordinamus, quod omnes, et singuli, qui absque dispensatione canonica, aut legitima licentia sive extra tempora a iure statuta . . . ad aliquem ex sacris ordinibus se fecerint promoveri, a suorum ordinum executione, ipso iure suspensi sint; et si huiusmodi suspensione durante, in eisdem ordinibus ministrare praesumpserint, eo ipso irregularitatem incurrant. Praetera . . . beneficiis ecclesiasticis possint iure privari."—*Fontes,* n. 57.

[24] "Nonnisi illae (poenae) quas in hac ipsa Constitutione inserimus eoque modo, quo inserimus, robur exinde habeant."—*Fontes,* n. 552.

[25] Canon 274, 4°.

CONCLUSIONS

1. Minor orders may be conferred at as many as four distinct ordination ceremonies; however, the Roman custom of separating the conferring of minor orders into two ceremonies is suggested as the most logical and best balanced division.

2. The computation of the time interval is a matter of choice and convenience. The liturgical or the civil calendar may be used according as they compute the interstice to the satisfaction of the Ordinary.

3. There is no strict obligation imposed on the ordinand of exercising the order received.

4. The intervention of the Bishop in shortening the intervals whenever he deems it necessary or useful to the Church is a true act of dispensation.

5. The conditions of necessity and utility may be personal as well as local, i.e., they may be present either in the candidate, or in the diocese in which he will serve.

6. The power to dispense as granted in canon 978 is conceded solely to the Bishop of Incardination. Only by special concession may the Ordaining Prelate dispense strangers presented to him for ordination with dimissorials.

7. The law of interstices (c. 978) must yield to the law which determines the canonical age for ordination (c. 975), and also to the law which fixes the course of studies required for ordination (c. 976), whenever there is conflict, for the reason that no dispensatory faculty is granted in the latter canons as it is conceded in the canon regarding the interstices.

8. There is no reason for tolerating contrary customs in regard to the interstices, even though such customs may enjoy a tolerated existence. *Epikeia* may be used in an emergency.

BIBLIOGRAPHY

Sources

Acta Apostolicae Sedis, Commentarium Officiale, Romae (Civitate Vaticana), 1909-

Acta et Decreta Sacrorum Conciliorum Recentiorum, Collectio Lacensis, 7 vols., Friburgi Brisgoviae: Herder and Co., 1870-1890,

Bullarum Diplomatum et Privilegiorum Sanctorum Romanorum Pontificum Taurinensis Editio, 25 vols., Augustae Taurinorum, 1857-1872.

Bullarii Romani Continuatio Summorum Pontificum, 19 vols., Prati, 1756-1883.

Codex Iuris Canonici Pii X Pontificis Maximi iussu digestus Benedicti XV auctoritate promulgatus, Romae: Typis Polyglottis Vaticanis, 1917. Reimpressio, 1934.

Codicis Iuris Canonici Fontes cura Emi Petri Card. Gasparri editi, 9 vols., Romae (postea Civitate Vaticana): Typis Polyglottis Vaticanis, 1923-1939. (Vols., VII-IX ed. cura et studio Emi Iustiniani Card. Serédi).

Corpus Iuris Canonici, ed. Lipsien. 2. post Aemilii Ludovici Richteri curas instruxit Aemilius Friedberg, 2 vols., Lipsiae: Ex Officina Bernhardi Tauchnitz, 1879-1881. Editio anastatice repetita, Lipsiae: Tauchnitz, 1922.

Decretales D. Gregorii Papae IX suae integritati una cum glossis restitutae, cum privilegio Gregorii XIII, Pont. Max., et aliorum Principum, Romae, 1582.

Decretum Gratiani emendatum et notationibus illustratum una cum glossis, Gregorii XIII, Pont. Max., iussu editum, 2 vols., Romae, 1582.

Jaffé, P., *Regesta Pontificum Romanorum ab condita Ecclesia ad annum post Christum natum MCXCVIII,* 2nd ed. (Kaltenbrunner, Ewald, Loewenfeld), 2 vols. in 1, Lipsiae, 1885-1888.

Pallottini, S., *Collectio Omnium Conclusionum et Resolutionum Quae in causis propositis apud Sacram Congregationem Cardinalium S. Concilii Tridentini Interpretum Prodierunt ab eius institutione anno MDLXIV ad annum MDCCCLX, distinctis titulis alphabetico ordine per materias digesta,* 18 vols., Romae, 1868-1895.

Potthast, A., *Regesta Pontificum Romanorum inde ab anno post Christum natum MCXCVIII ad annum MCCIV,* 2 vols., Berolini, 1874-1875.

Schroeder, H. J., *Canons and Decrees of the Council of Trent: Original text with English Translation,* St. Louis: B. Herder Book Co., 1941.

AUTHORS

Antonelli, Ioannes, *Tractatus Novissimus et Absolutissimus de Tempore Legali,* Venetiis, 1692.

Ayrinhac, H. A., *Legislation on the Sacraments in the New Code of Canon Law,* New York: Longmans, Green and Company, 1928.

[Bachofen], Charles Augustine, *A Commentary on the New Code of Canon Law,* 8 vols., St. Louis: B. Herder, Vol. IV, 3. ed., 1925.

Barbosa, Augustinus, *Pastoralis Sollicitudinis, sive De Officio et Potestate Episcopi tripartita descriptio,* Lugduni, 1656.

Beste, Udalricus, *Introductio in Codicem,* Collegeville, Minn.: St. John's Abbey Press, 1938.

Blat, Albertus, *Commentarium Textus Codicis Iuris Canonici,* 5 vols. in 6, Romae: F. Ferrari, 1921-1927.

Bonacina, Martinus, *Opera Omnia,* 3 vols., Venetiis, 1687.

Bouscaren, T. Lincoln, *The Canon Law Digest,* 2 vols., Milwaukee: The Bruce Publishing Co., 1934-1943.

Brys, J., *De Dispensatione in Iure Canonico,* Brugis: Beyaert, 1925.

Cappello, Felix, *Tractatus Canonico-Moralis de Sacramentis,* Vol. II, Pars III, *De Sacra Ordinatione,* Romae: Marietti, 1935.

Cicognani, Amleto Giovanni, *Canon Law,* Authorized English Version by O'Hara and Brennan, 2. ed., and rev., Philadelphia: Dolphin Press, 1935.

Coronata, Matthaeus Conte a, *Institutiones Iuris Canonici,* 5 vols., Taurini: Marietti, 1928-1936.

Devoti, Ioannes, *Institutionum Canonicarum Libri IV,* 2 vols., Gandae, 1836.

Dubé, Arthur Joseph, *The General Principles for the Reckoning of Time in Canon Law,* The Catholic University of America Canon Law Studies, n. 144, Washington, D. C.: The Catholic University of America Press, 1941.

Engel, Ludovicus, *Collegium Universi Iuris Canonici,* 9 ed., Beneventi, 1760.

Fagnanus, Prosper, *Jus Canonicum seu Commentaria Absolutissima in Quinque Libros Decretalium,* 5 vols., Romae, 1661.

Ferraris, F., *Prompta Bibliotheca, Canonica, Juridica, Moralis Theologica, necnon Ascetica, Polemica, Rubricistica, Historica,* 9 vols., Romae, 1885-1899.

Gasparri, P., *Tractatus Canonicus de Sacra Ordinatione,* 2 vols., Parisiis-Lugduni, 1893.

Gonzalez-Tellez, Emmanuel, *Commentaria Perpetua in Singulos Textus Quinque Librorum Decretalium Gregorii IX,* 5 vols., Venetiis, 1756.

Guilfoyle, Merlin Joseph, *Custom,* The Catholic University of America Canon Law Studies, n. 105, Washington, D. C.: The Catholic University of America, 1937.

Honorante, Romualdus, *Praxis Secretariae Tribunalis Cardinalis Urbis Vicarii,* 2. ed., Romae, 1762.

Keene, Michael James, *Religious Ordinaries and Canon 198,* The Catholic University of America Canon Law Studies, n. 135, Washington, D. C.: The Catholic University of America Press, 1942.

Many, S., *Praelectiones de Sacra Ordinatione,* Parisiis, 1905.

McBride, James Thomas, *Incardination and Excardination of Seculars,* The Catholic University of America Canon Law Studies, n. 145, Washington, D. C.: The Catholic University of America Press, 1941.

Michiels, P. G., *Normae Generales Iuris Canonici,* 2 vols., Lublin, Polonia: Universitas Catholica, 1929.

Noldin, Henricus, *Summa Theologiae Moralis,* 25. ed., recognita ab A. Schmitt, 3 vols., Oeniponte: Felician Rauch, 1938.

Pichler, Vitus, *Epitome Juris Canonici,* 2 vols., Venetiis, 1755.

Pirhing, Ehrenreich, *Jus Canonicum Nova Methodo Explicatum,* 5 vols. in 3, Dilingae, 1722.

Reiffenstuel, Anacletus, *Jus Canonicum Universum,* 5 vols. in 7, Parisiis, 1864-1870.

Reilly, Edward M., *The General Norms of Dispensation,* The Catholic University of America Canon Law Studies, n. 119, Washington, D. C.: The Catholic University of America Press, 1939.

Rufinus, *Summa Decretorum,* ed. H. Singer, Paderborn, 1902.

Schaefer, Timotheus, *De Religiosis ad Normam Codicis Iuris Canonici,* 3. ed., Romae: Typis Polyglottis Vaticanis, 1940.

Sebastianelli, Gulielmus, *Praelectiones Iuris Canonici, De Personis,* 2. ed., Romae: Pustet, 1905.

Schmalzgrueber, Franciscus, *Jus Ecclesiasticum Universum,* 5 vols. in 12, Romae, 1843-1845.

Suarez, F., *Opera Omnia,* 28 vols., ed. L. Vivés, Parisiis, 1856-1861.

Thomassinus, Ludovicus, *Vetus et Nova Ecclesiae Disciplina circa Beneficia et Beneficiarios,* 10 vols., Magontiaci, 1787.

Van Hove, A., *Commentarium Lovaniense in Codicem Iuris Canonici,* Vol. I, Tomus III, *De Consuetudine-De Temporis Supputatione,* Mechliniae: Dessain, 1933.

Vermeersch, Arthurus, et Creusen, Josephus, *Epitome Iuris Canonici,* Vol. II, 5. ed., Mechliniae-Romae: H. Dessain, 1934.

Wernz, Franciscus X., *Ius Decretalium,* 2. ed., 6 vols., Romae-Prati, 1906-1913.

Wernz, Franciscus, et Vidal, Petrus, *Ius Canonicum,* 7 toms. in 9 vols., Romae: Apud Aedes Universitatis Gregorianae, 1923-1938.

Periodical

Jurist, The, Washington, D. C., 1941-

BIOGRAPHICAL NOTE

John Mark Gannon was born April 27, 1916, at Erie, Pennsylvania. After completing his primary education in Saint Peter's Grade School, he entered the Cathedral Preparatory School in the same city. In 1933 he entered the preparatory seminary of Saint Charles College at Catonsville, Maryland. In 1935, he entered the North American College at Rome, Italy. After completion of his philosophical studies, he entered the Theological College of the Catholic University of America at Washington, D. C., where he received the degree of Licentiate in Sacred Theology in June, 1941. He was ordained to the Sacred Priesthood on May 22, 1941, at Saint Peter's Cathedral at Erie, Pennsylvania. In September of the same year he entered the Catholic University of America to pursue a course of studies in the School of Canon Law, from which he received the degree of Bachelor of Canon Law in May, 1942, and the degree of Licentiate in Canon Law in May, 1943.

ALPHABETICAL INDEX

CANON LAW STUDIES*

1. FRERIKS, REV. CELESTINE A., C.PP.S., J.C.D., Religious Congregations in Their External Relations, 121 pp., 1916.
2. GALLIHER, REV. DANIEL M., O.P., J.C.D., Canonical Elections, 117 pp., 1917.
3. BORKOWSKI, REV. AURELIUS L., O.F.M., J.C.D., De Confraternitatibus Ecclesiasticis, 136 pp., 1918.
4. CASTILLO, REV. CAYO, J.C.D., Disertacion Historico-Canonica sobre la Potestad del Cabildo en Sede Vacante o Impedida del Vicario Capitular, 99 pp., 1919 (1918).
5. KUBELBECK, REV. WILLIAM J., S.T.B., J.C.D., The Sacred Penitentiaria and Its Relation to Faculties of Ordinaries and Priests, 129 pp., 1918.
6. PETROVITS, REV. JOSEPH J. C., S.T.D., J.C.D., The New Church Law on Matrimony, X-461 pp., 1919.
7. HICKEY, REV. JOHN J., S.T.B., J.C.D., Irregularities and Simple Impediments in the New Code of Canon Law, 100 pp., 1920.
8. KLEKOTKA, REV. PETER J., S.T.B., J.C.D., Diocesan Consultors, 179 pp., 1920.
9. WANENMACHER, REV. FRANCIS, J.C.D., The Evidence in Ecclesiastical Procedure Affecting the Marriage Bond, 1920 (Printed 1935).
10. GOLDEN, REV. HENRY FRANCIS, J.C.D., Parochial Benefices in the New Code, IV-119 pp., 1921 (Printed 1925).
11. KOUDELKA, REV. CHARLES J., J.C.D., Pastors, Their Rights and Duties According to the New Code of Canon Law, 211 pp., 1921.
12. MELO, REV. ANTONIUS, O.F.M., J.C.D., De Exemptione Regularium, X-188 pp., 1921.
13. SCHAAF, REV. VALENTINE THEODORE, O.F.M., S.T.B., J.C.D., The Cloister, X-180 pp., 1921.
14. BURKE, REV. THOMAS JOSEPH, S.T.D., J.C.D., Competence in Ecclesiastical Tribunals, IV-117 pp., 1922.
15. LEECH, REV. GEORGE LEO, J.C.D., A Comparative Study of the Constitution "Apostolicae Sedis" and the "Codex Juris Canonici," 179 pp., 1922.
16. MOTRY, REV. HUBERT LOUIS, S.T.D., J.C.D., Diocesan Faculties According to the Code of Canon Law, II-167 pp., 1922.
17. MURPHY, REV. GEORGE LAWRENCE, J.C.D., Delinquencies and Penalties in the Administration and the Reception of the Sacraments, IV-121 pp., 1923.

* Below n. 100 only the following numbers are still available: Nn. 3, 4, 9, 25, 34, 57 and 75. Beginning with n. 100 only the following are unavailable: Nn. 100-111 inclusive, and n. 118.

18. O'Reilly, Rev. John Anthony, S.T.B., J.C.D., Ecclesiastical Sepulture in the New Code of Canon Law, 11-129 pp., 1923.
19. Michalicka, Rev. Wenceslas Cyril, O.S.B., J.C.D., Judicial Procedure in Dismissal of Clerical Exempt Religious, 107 pp., 1923.
20. Dargin, Rev. Edward Vincent, S.T.B., J.C.D., Reserved Cases According to the Code of Canon Law, IV-103 pp., 1924.
21. Godfrey, Rev. John A., S.T.B., J.C.D., The Right of Patronage According to the Code of Canon Law, 153 pp., 1924.
22. Hagedorn, Rev. Francis Edward, J.C.D., General Legislation on Indulgences, II-154 pp., 1924.
23. King, Rev. James Ignatius, J.C.D., The Administration of the Sacraments to Dying Non-Catholics, V-141 pp., 1924.
24. Winslow, Rev. Francis Joseph, O.F.M., J.C.D., Vicars and Prefects Apostolic, IV-149 pp., 1924.
25. Correa, Rev. Jose Servelion, S.T.L., J.C.D., La Potestad Legislativa de la Iglesia Catolica, IV-127 pp., 1925.
26. Dugan, Rev. Henry Francis, A.M., J.C.D., The Judiciary Department of the Diocesan Curia, 87 pp., 1925.
27. Keller, Rev. Charles Frederick, S.T.B., J.C.D., Mass Stipends, 167 pp., 1925.
28. Paschang, Rev. John Linus, J.C.D., The Sacramentals According to the Code of Canon Law, 129 pp., 1925.
29. Piontek, Rev. Cyrillus, O.F.M., S.T.B., J.C.D., De Indulto Exclaustrationis necnon Saecularizationis, XIII-289 pp., 1925.
30. Kearney, Rev. Richard Joseph, S.T.B., J.C.D., Sponsors at Baptism According to the Code of Canon Law, IV-127 pp., 1925.
31. Bartlett, Rev. Chester Joseph, A.M., LL.B., J.C.D., The Tenure of Parochial Property in the United States of America, V-108 pp., 1926.
32. Kilker, Rev. Adrian Jerome, J.C.D., Extreme Unction, V-425 pp., 1926.
33. McCormick, Rev. Robert Emmett, J.C.D., Confessors of Religious, VIII-266 pp., 1926.
34. Miller, Rev. Newton Thomas, J.C.D., Founded Masses According to the Code of Canon Law, VII-93 pp., 1926.
35. Roelker, Rev. Edward G., S.T.D., J.C.D., Principles of Privilege According to the Code of Canon Law, XI-166 pp., 1926.
36. Bakalarczyk, Rev. Richardus, M.I.C., J.U.D., De Novitiatu, VIII-208 pp., 1927.
37. Pizzuti, Rev. Lawrence, O.F.M., J.U.L., De Parochis Religiosis, 1927. (Not Printed.)
38. Bliley, Rev. Nicholas Martin, O.S.B., J.C.D., Altars According to the Code of Canon Law, XIX-132 pp., 1927.
39. Brown, Mr. Brendan Francis, A.B., LL.M., J.U.D., The Canonical Juristic Personality with Special Reference to its Status in the United States of America, V-212 pp., 1927.

40. CAVANAUGH, REV. WILLIAM THOMAS, C.P., J.U.D., The Reservation of the Blessed Sacrament, VIII-101 pp., 1927.
41. DOHENY, REV. WILLIAM J., C.S.C., A.B., J.U.D., Church Property: Modes of Acquisition, X-118 pp., 1927.
42. FELDHAUS, REV. ALOYSIUS H., C.PP.S., J.C.D., Oratories, IX-141 pp., 1927.
43. KELLY, REV. JAMES PATRICK, A.B., J.C.D., The Jurisdiction of the Simple Confessor, X-208 pp., 1927.
44. NEUBERGER, REV. NICHOLAS J., J.C.D., Canon 6 or the Relation of the Codex Juris Canonici to the Preceding Legislation, V-95 pp., 1927.
45. O'KEEFE, REV. GERALD MICHAEL, J.C.D., Matrimonial Dispensations, Powers of Bishops, Priests, and Confessors, VIII-232 pp., 1927.
46. QUIGLEY, REV. JOSEPH A. M., A.B., J.C.D., Condemned Societies, 139 pp., 1927.
47. ZAPLOTNIK, REV. JOHANNES LEO, J.C.D., De Vicariis Foraneis, X-142 pp., 1927.
48. DUSKIE, REV. JOHN ALOYSIUS, A.B., J.C.D., The Canonical Status of the Orientals in the United States, VIII-196 pp., 1928.
49. HYLAND, REV. FRANCIS EDWARD, J.C.D., Excommunication, Its Nature, Historical Development and Effects, VIII-181 pp., 1928.
50. REINMANN, REV. GERALD JOSEPH, O.M.C., J.C.D., The Third Order Secular of Saint Francis, 201 pp., 1928.
51. SCHENK, REV. FRANCIS J., J.C.D., The Matrimonial Impediments of Mixed Religion and Disparity of Cult, XVI-318 pp., 1929.
52. COADY, REV. JOHN JOSEPH, S.T.D., J.U.D., A.M., The Appointment of Pastors, VIII-150 pp., 1929.
53. KAY, REV. THOMAS HENRY, J.C.D., Competence in Matrimonial Procedure, VIII-164 pp., 1929.
54. TURNER, REV. SIDNEY JOSEPH, C.P., J.U.D., The Vow of Poverty, XLIX-217 pp., 1929.
55. KEARNEY, REV. RAYMOND A., A.B., S.T.D., J.C.D., The Principles of Delegation, VII-149 pp., 1929.
56. CONRAN, REV. EDWARD JAMES, A.B., J.C.D., The Interdict, V-163 pp., 1930.
57. O'NEILL, REV. WILLIAM H., J.C.D., Papal Rescripts of Favor, VII-218 pp., 1930.
58. BASTNAGEL, REV. CLEMENT VINCENT, J.U.D., The Appointment of Parochial Adjutants and Assistants, XV-257 pp., 1930.
59. FERRY, REV. WILLIAM A., A.B., J.C.D., Stole Fees, V-136 pp., 1930.
60. COSTELLO, REV. JOHN MICHAEL, A.B., J.C.D., Domicile and Quasi-Domicile, VII-201 pp., 1930.
61. KREMER, REV. MICHAEL NICHOLAS, A.B., S.T.B., J.C.D., Church Support in the United States, VI-136 pp., 1930.
62. ANGULO, REV. LUIS, C.M., J.C.D., Legislation de la Iglesia sobre la intencion en la application de la Santa Misa, VII-104 pp., 1931.

63. Frey, Rev. Wolfgang Norbert, O.S.B., A.B., J.C.D., The Act of Religious Profession, VIII-174 pp., 1931.
64. Roberts, Rev. James Brendan, A.B., J.C.D., The Banns of Marriage, XIV-140 pp., 1931.
65. Ryder, Rev. Raymond Aloysius, A.B., J.C.D., Simony, IX-151 pp., 1931.
66. Campagna, Rev. Angelo, Ph.D., J.U.D., Il Vicario Generale del Vescovo, VII-205 pp., 1931.
67. Cox, Rev. Joseph Godfrey, A.B., J.C.D., The Administration of Seminaries, VI-124 pp., 1931.
68. Gregory, Rev. Donald J., J.U.D., The Pauline Privilege, XV-165 pp., 1931.
69. Donohue, Rev. John F., J.C.D., The Impediment of Crime, VII-110 pp., 1931.
70. Dooley, Rev. Eugene A., O.M.I., J.C.D., Church Law on Sacred Relics, IX-143 pp., 1931.
71. Orth, Rev. Clement Raymond, O.M.C., J.C.D., The Approbation of Religious Institutes, 171 pp., 1931.
72. Pernicone, Rev. Joseph M., A.B., J.C.D., The Ecclesiastical Prohibition of Books, XII-267 pp., 1932.
73. Clinton, Rev. Connell, A.B., J.C.D., The Paschal Precept, IX-108 pp., 1932.
74. Donnelly, Rev. Francis B,. A.M., S.T.L., J.C.D., The Diocesan Synod, VIII-125 pp., 1932.
75. Torrente, Rev. Camilo, C.M.F., J.C.D., Las Procesiones Sagradas, V-145 pp., 1932.
76. Murphy, Rev. Edwin J., C.PP.S., J.C.D., Suspension Ex Informata Conscientia, XI-122 pp., 1932.
77. MacKenzie, Rev. Eric F., A.M., S.T.L., J.C.D., The Delict of Heresy in its Commission, Penalization, Absolution, VII-124 pp., 1932.
78. Lyons, Rev. Avitus E., S.T.B., J.C.D., The Collegiate Tribunal of First Instance, XI-147 pp., 1932.
79. Connolly, Rev. Thomas A., J.C.D., Appeals, XI-195 pp., 1932.
80. Sangmeister, Rev. Joseph V., A.B., J.C.D., Force and Fear as Precluding Matrimonial Consent, V-211 pp., 1932.
81. Jaeger, Rev. Leo A., A.B., J.C.D., The Administration of Vacant and Quasi-Vacant Episcopal Sees in the United States, IX-229 pp., 1932.
82. Rimlinger, Rev. Herbert T., J.C.D., Error Invalidating Matrimonial Consent, VII-79 pp., 1932.
83. Barrett, Rev. John D. M., S.S., J.C.D., A Comparative Study of the Third Plenary Council of Baltimore and the Code, IX-221 pp., 1932.
84. Carberry, Rev. John J., Ph.D., S.T.D., J.C.D., The Juridical Form of Marriage, X-177 pp., 1934.
85. Dolan, Rev. John L., A.B., J.C.D., The Defensor Vinculi, XII-157 pp., 1934.

86. HANNAN, REV. JEROME D., A.M., S.T.D., LL.B., J.C.D., The Canon Law of Wills, IX-517 pp., 1934.
87. LEMIEUX, REV. DELISE A., A.M., J.C.D., The Sentence in Ecclesiastical Procedure, IX-131 pp., 1934.
88. O'ROURKE, REV. JAMES J., A.B., J.C.D., Parish Registers, VII-109 pp., 1934.
89. TIMLIN, REV. BARTHOLOMEW, O.F.M., A.M., J.C.D., Conditional Matrimonial Consent, X-381 pp., 1934.
90. WAHL, REV. FRANCIS X., A.B., J.C.D., The Matrimonial Impediments of Consanguinity and Affinity, VI-125 pp., 1934.
91. WHITE, REV. ROBERT J., A.B., LL.B., S.T.B., J.C.D., Canonical Ante-Nuptial Promises and the Civil Law, VI-152 pp., 1934.
92. HERRERA, REV. ANTONIO PARRA, O.C.D., J.C.D., Legislacion Ecclesiastica sobra el Ayuno y la Abstinencia, XI-191 pp., 1935.
93. KENNEDY, REV. EDWIN J., J.C.D., The Special Matrimonial Process in Cases of Evident Nullity, X-165 pp., 1935.
94. MANNING, REV. JOHN J., A.B., J.C.D., Presumption of Law in Matrimonial Procedure, XI-111 pp., 1935.
95. MOEDER, REV. JOHN M., J.C.D., The Proper Bishop for Ordination and Dimissorial Letters, VII-135 pp., 1935.
96. O'MARA, REV. WILLIAM A., A.B., J.C.D., Canonical Causes for Matrimonial Dispensations, IX-155 pp., 1935.
97. REILLY, REV. PETER, J.C.D., Residence of Pastors, IX-81 pp., 1935.
98. SMITH, REV. MARINER T., O.P., S.T.Lr., J.C.D., The Penal Law for Religious, VII-169 pp., 1935.
99. WHALEN, REV. DONALD W., A.M., J.C.D., The Value of Testimonial Evidence in Matrimonial Procedure, XIII-297 pp., 1935.
100. CLEARY, REV. JOSEPH F., J.C.D., Canonical Limitations on the Alienation of Church Property, VIII-141 pp., 1936.
101. GLYNN, REV. JOHN C., J.C.D., The Promoter of Justice, XX-337 pp., 1936.
102. BRENNAN, REV. JAMES H., S.S., M.A., S.T.B., J.C.D., The Simple Convalidation of Marriage, VI-135 pp., 1937.
103. BBUNINI, REV. JOSEPH BERNARD, J.C.D., The Clerical Obligations of Canons 139 and 142, X-121 pp., 1937.
104. CONNOR, REV. MAURICE, A.B., J.C.D., The Administrative Removal of Pastors, VIII-159 pp., 1937.
105. GUILFOYLE, REV. MERLIN JOSEPH, J.C.D., Custom, XI-144 pp., 1937.
106. HUGHES, REV. JAMES AUSTIN, A.B., A.M., J.C.D., Witnesses in Criminal Trials of Clerics, IX-140 pp., 1937.
107. JANSEN, REV. RAYMOND J., A.B., S.T.L., J.C.D., Canonical Provisions for Catechetical Instruction, VII-153 pp., 1937.
108. KEALY, REV. JOHN JAMES, A.B., J.C.D., The Introductory Libellus in Church Court Procedure, XI-121 pp., 1937.
109. MCMANUS, REV. JAMES EDWARD, C.SS.R., J.C.D., The Administration of Temporal Goods in Religious Institutes, XVI-196 pp., 1937.

110. MORIARTY, REV. EUGENE JAMES, J.C.D., Oaths in Ecclesiastical Courts, X-115 pp., 1937.
111. RAINER, REV. ELIGIUS GEORGE, C.SS.R., J.C.D., Suspension of Clerics, XVII-249 pp., 1937.
112. REILLY, REV. THOMAS F., C.SS.R., J.C.D., Visitation of Religious, VI-195 pp., 1938.
113. MORIARITY, REV. FRANCIS E., C.SS.R., J.C.D., The Extraordinary Absolution from Censures, XV-334 pp., 1938.
114. CONNOLLY, REV. NICHOLAS P., J.C.D., The Canonical Erection of Parishes, X-132 pp., 1938.
115. DONOVAN, REV. JAMES JOSEPH, J.C.D., The Pastor's Obligation in Prenuptial Investigation, XII-322 pp., 1938.
116. HARRIGAN, REV. ROBERT J., M.A., S.T.B., J.C.D., The Radical Sanation of Invalid Marriages, VIII-208 pp., 1938.
117. BOFFA, REV. CONRAD HUMBERT, J.C.D., Canonical Provisions for Catholic Schools, VII-211 pp., 1939.
118. PARSONS, REV. ANSCAR JOHN, O.M.Cap., J.C.D., Canonical Elections, XII-236 pp., 1939.
119. REILLY, REV. EDWARD MICHAEL, A.B., J.C.D., The General Norms of Dispensation, XII-156 pp., 1939.
120. RYAN, REV. GERALD ALOYSIUS, A.B., J.C.D., Principles of Episcopal Jurisdiction, XII-172 pp., 1939.
121. BURTON, REV. FRANCIS JAMES, C.S.C., A.B., J.C.D., A Commentary on Canon 1125, X-222 pp., 1940.
122. MIASKIEWICZ, REV. FRANCIS SIGISMUND, J.C.D., Supplied Jurisdiction According to Canon 209, XII-340 pp., 1940.
123. RICE, REV. PATRICK WILLIAM, A.B., J.C.D., Proof of Death in Prenuptial Investigation, VIII-156 pp., 1940.
124. ANGLIN, REV. THOMAS FRANCIS, M.S., J.C.D., The Eucharistic Fast, VIII-183 pp., 1941.
125. COLEMAN, REV. JOHN JEROME, J.C.D., The Minister of Confirmation, VI-153 pp., 1941.
126. DOWNS, REV. JOSEPH EMMANUEL, A.B., J.C.D., The Concept of Clerical Immunity, XI-163 pp., 1941.
127. ESSWEIN, REV. ANTHONY ALBERT, J.C.D., Extrajudicial Penal Powers of Ecclesiastical Superiors, X-144 pp., 1941.
128. FARRELL, REV. BENJAMIN FRANCIS, M.A., S.T.L., J.C.D., The Rights and Duties of the Local Ordinary Regarding Congregations of Women Religious of Pontifical Approval, V-195 pp., 1941.
129. FEENEY, REV. THOMAS JOHN, A.B., S.T.L., J.C.D., Restitutio in Integrum, VI-169 pp., 1941.
130. FINDLAY, REV. STEPHEN WILLIAM, O.S.B., A.B., J.C.D., Canonical Norms Governing the Deposition and Degradation of Clerics, XVII-279 pp., 1941.
131. GOODWINE, REV. JOHN, A.B., S.T.L., J.C.D., The Right of the Church to Acquire Property, VIII-119 pp., 1941.

132. Heston, Rev. Edward Louis, C.S.C., Ph.D., S.T.D., J.C.D., The Alienation of Church Property in the United States, XII-222 pp., 1941.
133. Hogan, Rev. James John, A.B., S.T.L., J.C.D., Judicial Advocates and Procurators, XIII-200 pp., 1941.
134. Kealy, Rev. Thomas M., A.B., Litt.D., J.C.D., Dowry of Women Religious, IX-152 pp., 1941.
135. Keene, Rev. Michael James, O.S.B., J.C.D., Religious Ordinaries and Canon 198, V-164 pp., 1942.
136. Kerin, Rev. Charles A., S.S., M.A., S.T.B., J.C.D., The Privation of Christian Burial, XVI-279 pp., 1941.
137. Louis, Rev. William Francis, M.A., J.C.D., Diocesan Archives, X-101 pp., 1941.
138. McDevitt, Rev. Gilbert Joseph, A.B., J.C.D., Legitimacy and Legitimation, X-247 pp., 1941.
139. McDonough, Rev. Thomas Joseph, A.B., J.C.D., Apostolic Administrators, X-217 pp., 1941.
140. Meier, Rev. Carl Anthony, A.B., J.C.D., Penal Administration Procedure Against Negligent Pastors, XI-240 pp., 1941.
141. Schmidt, Rev. John Rogg, A.B., J.C.D., The Principles of Authentic Interpretation in Canon 17 of the Code of Canon Law, XII-331 pp., 1941.
142. Slafkosky, Rev. Andrew Leonard, A.B., J.C.D., The Canonical Episcopal Visitation of the Diocese, X-197 pp., 1941.
143. Swoboda, Rev. Innocent Robert, O.F.M., J.C.D., Ignorance in Relation to the Imputability of Delicts, IX-271 pp., 1941.
144. Dubé, Rev. Arthur Joseph, A.B., J.C.D., The General Principles for the Reckoning of Time in Canon Law, VIII-299 pp., 1941.
145. McBride, Rev. James T., A.B., J.C.D., Incardination and Excardination of Seculars, XX-585 pp., 1941.
146. Krol, Rev. John T., J.C.D., The Defendant in Ecclesiastical Trials, XII-207 pp., 1942.
147. Comyns, Rev. Joseph J., C.SS.R., A.B., J.C.D., Papal and Episcopal Administration of Church Property, XIV-155 pp., 1942.
148. Barry, Rev. Garrett Francis, O.M.I., J.C.D., Violation of the Cloister, XII-260 pp., 1942.
149. Bolduc, Rev. Gatien, C.S.V., A.B., S.T.L., J.C.D., Les Études dans les Religions Cléricales, VIII-155 pp., 1942.
150. Boyle, Rev. David John, M.A., J.C.D., The Juridic Effects of Moral Certitude on Pre-Nuptial Guarantees, XII-188 pp., 1942.
151. Canavan, Rev. Walter Joseph, M.A., Litt.D., J.C.D., The Profession of Faith, XII-143 pp., 1942.
152. Desrochers, Rev. Bruno, A.B., Ph.L., S.T.B., J.C.D., Le Premier Concile Plénier de Québec et le Code de Droit Canonique, XIV-186 pp., 1942.

153. DILLON, REV. ROBERT EDWARD, A.B., J.C.D., Common Law Marriage, X-148 pp., 1942.
154. DODWELL, REV. EDWARD JOHN, PH.D., S.T.B., J.C.D., The Time and Place for the Celebration of Marriage, X-156 pp., 1942.
155. DONNELLAN, REV. THOMAS ANDREW, A.B., J.C.D., The Obligation of the Misa pro Populo, VII-131 pp., 1942.
156. ELTZ, REV. LOUIS ANTHONY, A.B., J.C.L., Cooperation in Crime.
157. GASS, REV. SYLVESTER FRANCIS, M.A., J.C.D., Ecclesiastical Pensions, XI-206 pp., 1942.
158. GUINIVEN, REV. JOHN JOSEPH, C.SS.R., J.C.D., The Precept of Hearing Mass, XIV-188 pp., 1942.
159. GULCZYNSKI, REV. JOHN THEOPHILUS, J.C.D., The Desecration and Violation of Churches, X-126 pp., 1942.
160. HAMMILL, REV. JOHN LEO, M.A., J.C.D., The Obligations of the Traveler According to Canon 14, VIII-204 pp., 1942.
161. HAYDT, REV. JOHN JOSEPH, A.B., J.C.D., Reserved Benefices, XI-148 pp., 1942.
162. HUSER, REV. ROGER JOHN, O.F.M., A.B., J.C.D., The Crime of Abortion in Canon Law, XII-187 pp., 1942.
163. KEARNEY, REV. FRANCIS PATRICK, A.B., S.T.L., J.C.L., The Principles of Canon 1127
164. LINAHEN, REV. LEO JAMES, S.T.L., J.C.D., De Absolutione Complicis In Peccato Turpi, 114 pp., 1942.
165. MCCLOSKEY, REV. JOSEPH ALOYSIUS, A.B., J.C.D., The Subject of Ecclesiastical Law According to Canon 12, XVII-246 pp., 1942.
166. O'NEILL, REV. FRANCIS JOSEPH, C.SS.R., J.C.D., The Dismissal of Religious in Temporary Vows, XIII-220 pp., 1942.
167. PRINCE, REV. JOHN EDWARD, A.B., S.T.D., J.C.D., The Diocesan Chancellor, X-136 pp., 1942.
168. RIESNER, REV. ALBERT JOSEPH, C.SS.R., J.C.D., Apostates and Fugitives from Religious Institutes, IX-168 pp., 1942.
169. STENGER, REV. JOSEPH BERNARD, J.C.D., The Mortgaging of Church Property, 186 pp., 1942.
170. WALDRON, REV. JOSEPH FRANCIS, A.B., J.C.D., The Minister of Baptism, XII-197 pp., 1942.
171. WILLETT, REV. ROBERT ALBERT, J.C.D., The Probative Value of Documents in Ecclesiastical Trials, X-124 pp., 1942.
172. WOEBER, REV. EDWARD MARTIN, M.A., J.C.D., The Interpellations, XII-161 pp., 1942.
173. BENKO, REV. MATTHEW ALOYSIUS, O.S.B., M.A., J.C.L., The Abbot *Nullius*.
174. CHRIST, REV. JOSEPH JAMES, M.A., S.T.L., J.C.L., Dispensation from Vindicative Penalties.
175. CLANCY, REV. PATRICK M. J., O.P., A.B., S.T.LR., J.C.D., The Local Religious Superior, X-299 pp., 1943.

176. Clarke, Rev. Thomas James, J.C.D., Parish Societies, XII-147 pp., 1943.
177. Connolly, Rev. John Patrick, S.T.L., J.C.D., Synodal Examiners and Parish Priest Consultors, X-223 pp., 1943.
178. Drumm, Rev. William Martin, A.B., J.C.L., Hospital Chaplains.
179. Flanagan, Rev. Bernard Joseph, A.B., S.T.L., J.C.D., The Canonical Erection of Religious Houses, X-147 pp., 1943.
180. Kelleher, Rev. Stephen Joseph, A.B., S.T.B., J.C.D., Discussions with non-Catholics: Canonical Legislation, X-93 pp., 1943.
181. Lewis, Rev. Gordian, C.P., J.C.D., Chapters in Religious Institutes, XII-169 pp., 1943.
182. Marx, Rev. Adolph, J.C.D., The Declaration of Nullity of Marriages Contracted Outside the Church, X-151 pp., 1943.
183. Matulenas, Rev. Raymond Anthony, O.S.B., A.B., J.C.L., Communication, a Source of Privileges.
184. O'Leary, Rev. Charles Gerard, C.SS.R., J.C.D., Religious Dismissed After Perpetual Profession, X-213 pp., 1943.
185. Power, Rev. Cornelius Michael, J.C.L., The Blessing of Cemeteries.
186. Shuhler, Rev. Ralph Vincent, O.S.A., J.C.D., Privileges of Regulars to Absolve and Dispense, XII-195 pp., 1943.
187. Ziolkowski, Rev. Thaddeus Stanislaus, A.B., J.C.D., The Consecration and Blessing of Churches, XII-151 pp., 1943.
188. Heneghan, Rev. John Joseph, S.T.D., J.C.L., The Marriages of Unworthy Catholics: Canons 1065 and 1066.
189. Carroll, Rev. Coleman Francis, M.A., S.T.L., J.C.L., Charitable Institutions.
190. Ciesluk, Rev. Joseph Edward, Ph.B., S.T.L., J.C.L., National Parishes in the United States.
191. Coburn, Rev. Vincent Paul, A.B., J.C.L., Marriages of Conscience.
192. Connors, Rev. Charles Paul, C.S.Sp., A.B., J.C.L., Extra-Judicial Procurators in the Code of Canon Law.
193. Coyle, Rev. Paul Raymond, A.B., J.C.L., Judicial Exceptions.
194. Fair, Rev. Bartholomew Francis, A.B., S.T.L., J.C.L., The Impediment of Abduction.
195. Gallagher, Rev. Thomas Raphael, O.P., A.B., S.T.Lr., J.C.L., The Examination of the Qualities of the Ordinand.
196. Gannon, Rev. John Mark, S.T.L., J.C.L., The Interstices Required for the Promotion to Orders.
197. Goldsmith, Rev. J. William, B.C.S., S.T.L., J.C.L., The Competence of Church and State over Marriage—Disputed Points.
198. Goodwine, Rev. Joseph Gerard, A.B., S.T.B., J.C.L., The Reception of Converts.
199. Kowalski, Rev. Romuald Eugene, O.F.M., A.B., J.C.L., Sustenance of Religious Houses of Regulars.
200. McCoy, Rev. Alan Edward, O.F.M., J.C.L., Force and Fear in Relation to Delictual Imputability and Penal Responsibility.

201. McDevitt, Rev. Vincent John, Ph.B., S.T.L., J.C.L., Perjury.
202. Martin, Rev. Thomas Owen, Ph.D., S.T.D., J.C.L., Adverse Possession, Prescription and Limitation of Actions: The Canonical "Praescriptio."
203. Miklosovic, Rev. Paul John, A.B., J.C.L., Attempted Marriages and Their Consequent Juridic Effects.
204. Mundy, Rev. Thomas Maurice, A.B., S.T.L., J.C.L., The Union of Parishes.
205. O'Dea, Rev. John Coyle, A.B., J.C.L., The Matrimonial Impediment of Nonage.
206. Olalia, Rev. Alexander Ayson, S.T.L., J.C.L., A Comparative Study of the Christian Constitution of States and the Constitution of the Philippine Commonwealth.
207. Poisson, Rev. Pierre-Marie, C.S.C., A.B., Ph.L., Th.L., J.C.L., Droits Patrimoniaux des Maisons et des Eglises Religieuses.
208. Stadalnikas, Rev. Casimir Joseph, M.I.C., J.C.L., Reservation of Censures.
209. Sullivan, Rev. Eugene Henry, S.T.L., J.C.L., Proof of the Reception of the Sacraments.
210. Vaughan, Rev. William Edward, J.C.L., Constitutions for Diocesan Courts.
211. Lyons, Rev. Joseph Henry, J.C.L., The Joinder of Issue in Canonical Trials.

www.ingramcontent.com/pod-product-compliance
Lightning Source LLC
LaVergne TN
LVHW050200080826
844660LV00012B/320

* 9 7 8 0 8 1 3 2 2 3 8 3 4 *